THE REFORM OF THE UNITED NATIONS

THE CROOM HELM UNITED NATIONS AND ITS
AGENCIES SERIES
Edited by David Pitt and Thomas Weiss

*THE NATURE OF THE UNITED NATIONS
BUREAUCRACIES*
Edited by David Pitt and Thomas Weiss

REFUGEES IN INTERNATIONAL POLITICS
Leon Gordenker

The Reform of the United Nations

DAVID STEELE

CROOM HELM
London • Sydney • Wolfeboro, New Hampshire

© 1987 David Steele
Croom Helm Ltd, Provident House, Burrell Row,
Beckenham, Kent, BR3 1AT
Croom Helm Australia, 44-50 Waterloo Road,
North Ryde, 2113, New South Wales

British Library Cataloguing in Publication Data

Steele, David
    The reform of the United Nations.
    1. United Nations
    I. Title
    341.23   JX1977

    ISBN 0-7099-4480-2

Croom Helm, 27 South Main Street,
Wolfeboro, New Hampshire 03894-2069, USA

Library of Congress Cataloging-in-Publication Data

Steele, David, 1934-
    The reform of the United Nations.

    1. United Nations. 2. Security, International.
3. Rural development. I. Title.
JX1977.S76   1987   341.23   86-24373
ISBN 0-7099-4480-2

Printed and bound in Great Britain by Mackays of Chatham Ltd, Kent

Contents

List of Tables
List of Figures
List of Abbreviations
Preface
     INTRODUCTION 1

1. WHY THE UNITED NATIONS SYSTEM IS MORE THAN
   EVER NEEDED 3

     Insure States Against Aggression 5
     Protect the Individual Against Abuses
       of Human Rights 6
     Steadying and Regulating the Global Economy 8
     Rectify Global Inequalities 11
     Preserve the Common Heritage of all Mankind 13
     Safeguard Interests of Future Generations 13
     Promote Appropriate Social and Economic
       Development 14
     Peaceful Resolution of Inter-state Disputes 14

2. REFORMING THE UN IS NOT EASY 16

     Problems Expand, the System Grows but Cannot
       Keep Pace 16
     History of Minor Reforms 19
       Reforms Arising from the Arrival of the
         Developing Countries in the UN 20
       Reforms to Improve Coordination 20
       Reforms Responding to the Blockage in
         the Security Council 22
     Escaping from the Dilemma of Attainable
       and Irrelevant or Radical but
       Unattainable Reforms 23
       The Institutionalisation of the Power of
         National Sovereignty 23

It will be difficult to Reform the
    Charter 25
The Agencies Have an Interest in the
    Status-quo 26
Only in a Period of Detente can
    Progress be Made 27
Many Governments and the Secretary
    General Have at Most a Medium Term
    Time Horizon 29
Many People and Powerful Interest
    Groups May Take a More Localised
    or Conservative View than their
    Governments on Global Issues 29
A Process which can Raise the Ceiling of
    Reform Objectives 30
How Much Compromise to Preserve
    Universality 31
Common Institutional Solutions Linking the
    Major Global Issues 32
There is No Resolution of the Balance
    of Voting in the System to Allow
    Effective Control 32
Insufficient Committment to Issues
    and System Structure Make for a
    Conservative Response to Programme
    Financing 33
Technical Complexity Requires Either
    Effective Methods of Coordination or
    Decentralisation 36
Temporary and Medium Level Political
    Country Representatives Cannot Control
    the Secretariats of the UN and
    Agencies 37
The Agencies have Major Types of
    Activity in Common 38
Three Problem Areas which Isolate Common
    Institutional Solutions 39

3.   PROBLEM AREA ONE: GLOBAL ECONOMIC MANAGEMENT 44

The Extent of the Economic Problem 46
The Financial Crisis 46
A Derived Crisis 47
The Limits of Global Economic Institutions 49
The Concept of Global Economic Management 50
Reviews and Forecasting 52
Forums for Decision on GEM 53
The GEM Process 54
GEM Formulation Conference 55
GEM Decision Making 56
Secretariat Rationalisation for the GEM
    Process 59

Implications for the United Nations 61
Impact of GEM on Growth and Development.   63

4. PROBLEM AREA TWO: RURAL DEVELOPMENT AND THE
    ENVIRONMENT 67

    Scale of Rural Development Problems   69
    Structure and Policy Focus of United
      Nations System Agencies   71
    Are the Representative Bodies Blocking
      Rural Poverty Oriented Programmes? ...   75
    Do Policy Coordination Mechanisms for
      Rural Development Function?   79
      Coordination at the Country Level   80
      Has Joint Programming Worked?   82
    Towards More Effective Coordination   85
      A Summary of Current Coordination
        Difficulties   85
      Too many Problems in an Uncontrolled
        Multi-agency System   86
      Can the United Nations Coordinate with
        or Control the World Bank Group?   86
      A United Nations System Wide Planning
        Cycle   87
      Joint Programming as a Role for the
        Regional Commissions   88
      Coordination through Medium Term Plans   88
      Coordination through Budgets, Secretariat
        Line Control and through Agency
        Representative Bodies   89
    A new Strategy of Technical Cooperation .   91
      RRUNDP to interpret United Nations System
        Policy at the Country Level   91
      Support from Country Coordination
        Ministries   92
      Country System wide Programming   93
    Summary   94

5. PROBLEM AREA THREE: THIRD WORLD COLLECTIVE
    SECURITY AND DISARMAMENT   97

    Background   97
    Peace and Security Issues in the UN under
      the Charter: Past Problems and Recent
      Developments 100
      Powers of the General Assembly in Peace
        and Security Matters 100
      Appeals by the Secretary-General and
        Response of the General Assembly and
        the Security Council 103
    Political Realities and Possible Outcomes 105
      Security Council or General Assembly . 105

Is a cost of Collective Security the
   Slowing Down of Political Change?   106
Conditions for a Significant Reform of
   the Security Council   109
A Proposal to Make a Permanent Commission
   of the Security Council   111
   Essential Tasks of a Security Council
      Permanent Commission   111
   How Would the Commission Differ from the
      Security Council Itself?   112
   How Would Commissioners be Chosen? ...   113
   How Would Commissioners Function in
      Relation to the Secretariat?   113
The Range of Activities of the Commission   114
   Information Gathering   114
   Peaceful Settlement of Disputes   116
   Economic Sanctions   119
   Strengthening of Regional Pacts of
      Collective Security   121
   Peace-keeping and Enforcement   122
   Disarmament   123
Costing of the Commission   125
   Costs   125
   Funding   126
Summary   129

6.   CONCLUSION   136

Existing Balances of Power   136
A United Nations which Avoids both Undue
   Heterogeneity as well as Monolithism .   140
Weighing the Politics Behind the Options
   for Reform   142
Existing Suggestions for General
   Assembly Reform   150
The Agencies have to Submit to United
   Nations System Wide Policy   153
Plausible Reform Options   156
   Theoretically Different Basis for a UN   156
   Charter Reforms   158
   Reforms Within the Charter   160
Are We Heading Towards or Even Aiming at
   Supranationality?   162
Feasible Pathways   165
Raising Public Consciousness and Putting
   the Process of Reform in Motion   165

Annex 1   Rough costing of the work of the
             Security Council Commission   171
      2   Draft Collective Security and
             Disarmament Agreement   173

TABLES AND FIGURES

Tables

1.1   Share of Exports in GDP..................   9
2.1   The Top Ten Contributors to the UN 1985
       Regular Budget   34
4.1   Balance of Voting by World Bank Country
       Groups in the Governing Bodies of the
       UN System Agencies 1983/4   76
5.1   Budget and Staff of the United Nations
       Organs Concerned with Peace and Security
       for Biennium 1984/85   127
5.2   Rough Costing of the Security Council
       Peace and Security Commission   128
6.1   Alternative Weighted Voting Systems and
       their Impact on Majorities in a General
       Assembly Resolution   151
Annex 2.1 :Disarmament Programme   177

Figures

5.1   Peaceful Settlement of Disputes Process..   118
6.1   Existing Balance of Power in the UN......   137
6.2   A Possible Timeframe for Reforms   166

Abbreviations

ACC	Administrative Committee on Coordination
CCSQ	Consultative Committee on Substantive Questions
CMEA	Council for Mutual Economic Assistance
CPC	Committee for Programme Coordination
DIESA	Department for International Economic and Social Affairs
ECOSOC	Economic and Social Council
ECSC	European Coal and Steel Community
EEC	European Economic Community
FAO	Food and Agriculture Organisation
FICSA	Federation of International Civil Servants Association
GATT	General Agreement on Tariffs and Trade
GDP	gross domestic product
GEM	global economic management
GNP	gross national product
IAEA	International Atomic Energy Agency
ICJ	International Court of Justice
ICSC	International Civil Servants Association
IDA	International Development Association
IFAD	International Fund for Agricultural Development
ILO	International Labour Organisation
IMF	International Monetary Fund
INTERPOL	International Criminal Police Organisation
ITO	International Trade Organisation
JIU	Joint Inspection Unit
NGO	non-governmant organisation
NIEO	New International Economic Order

OECD	Organisation for Economic Cooperation and Development
PHC	primary health care
RRUNDP	resident representative of the UNDP
SDR	special drawing rights
SUNFED	Special UN Fund for Economic Development
TNC	trans-national corporations
UN	United Nations
UNCTAD	UN Conference on Trade Aid and Development
UNDOF	UN Disengagement Observer Force
UNDP	UN Development Programme
UNEF	UN Emergency Force
UNEP	UN Environment Programme
UNESCO	UN Educational, Scientific and Cultural Organisation
UNFICYP	UN Peace-keeping Force in Cyprus
UNFPA	UN Fund for Population Activities
UNICEF	UN Children's Fund
UNIDO	UN Industrial Development Organisation
UNIFIL	UN International Force in Lebanon
UNITAR	UN Institute for Training and Research
US	United States of America
USSR	Union of Soviet Socialist Republics
WCARRD	World Conference on Agrarian Reform and Rural Development
WFP	World Food Programme
WHO	World Health Organisation

PREFACE

Some professional writers can turn out a fair weight of books in their life span. Public servants sometimes manage one or two. Time in their working life is at a premium and in their retirement, rose growing or its equivalent has the priority. As I still claim to be in my 'prime', I must express my gratitude to the UN System for providing the time if not the encouragement to write this book, the contents of which of course cannot be ascribed to anyone except myself. Also absolved from any blame or come back are the EDP team of UNICEF, the UN, Research Institutes for Social Development, and of course WHO.

To write a book on UN reform, it was certainly useful to have worked in different parts of the System over a long period. Its complexity clouds many students either into simplistic recommendations or to a surrender to the continuation of the status quo. By and large, the second group has example on its side.

The web of political balance overlying the UN Charter and UN Agency constitutional niceties have both developed organically over the forty years of the System's growth since 1947 and this is not at all a bad thing to have happened. There are two reasons why it is necessary to probe into the morass and attempt to produce a change for the better, if not a complete surgical cure. The first is that the System's growth has been uncontrolled and without direction and like a stranded dinosaur, is now in danger of becoming irrelevant to the demands of its environment. The second is that the stress between the major actors in the System has grown too great to sustain the balances that were attempted, but never really applied in the past. There is no longer an acceptable balance of political forces, or rather there is again a great imbalance. In the early years of the UN, the major imbalance was perceived by the USSR and then, although the UN did not blow apart, it functioned as if it had both hands tied behind its back. Although the perception of imbalance has merely switched to the other superpower block, the world has grown both more complex and more dangerous. The world needs now a well working UN System so much more than in its early years.

The UN is seen in this book as a play with five actors. First, there are the representatives of governments who are supposed to control and direct. Second, there is the Secretariat; third are the non-government organisations which sometimes for the benefit of all and sometimes in their own interest, put pressure on the important representative meetings. Fourth is the broad mass of the general public which is informed or not about the happenings and potential of the UN and has been only very weakly able to respond. Fifth and last there are the autonomous and semi-autonomous agencies within the UN System.

The most complex group of actors to understand are the representatives. The first distinction to draw is between the civil servants which represent governments who have considerable latitude in their specialised areas and the politicians or high ranking politicised civil servants that stand behind them if the issues reach that level. The question is asked whether there is something in the make-up of a large number of modern governments that they have such a lack of interest in global long term solutions to world problems. What does it imply for the future, maintaining governments as the strong partner in the System?

Next, still within the group of representatives, is the distinction between the blocks. There are the two superpowers, the USSR and the US, around whom there are grouped a number of other supportive satellite governments. There are the block of western industrialised countries, called here the North West. The socialist East includes not only the satellites of the USSR but all the European socialist countries and those of the developing countries. The developing South group, formalised in group of '77' block meetings, is broadly synonymous with the non-aligned, although the number of non-aligned in fact has reduced, as the superpowers have persuaded more countries to their camp. There are other groups of occasional importance, partly based on regions, such as the Pacific block, the African, Latin American, Asian and European Economic Community.

The Secretariat in the early days was thought of as an international civil service. This idea has been diluted but not totally lost. It has been dissipated partly as a result of the distrust of the UN by the USSR and other socialist countries which kept their serving officers on short duties with the UN and Agencies and partly because of over rapid recruitment without certainty of commitment or education for the task. Finding technical specialists with global understanding and commitment was not so easy. It is also important to appreciate that power lies in the Secretariat at the levels of the Director Generals of the Agencies and for both the UN and the Agencies, at the level of the Directors and the Programme Managers.

The non-government organisations (NGO's) are of two types. Some NGO's are actually accredited to the UN and the Agencies and are graded in importance and rights. The important ones can raise issues for debate and can speak at meetings when called upon. NGO's hold mini-conferences before major inter-governmental UN meetings and can influence them somewhat by their pressure. The second type are the partial sectoral interest groups which are also sometimes very influential and often negatively so. An exception is in the tripartite ILO assemblies where the employers and workers organisations by and large have over a long period been educated up to public spirited attitudes and oppositions are subtly expressed.

The general public can attend public meetings and open days, use the UN and Agency libraries, ask for information from the Secretariat, and are from time to time informed of the important events through the press or from published media, mainly publications. They may be the direct beneficaries of development programmes. Members of the general public cannot directly address the UN bodies but they can make individual human rights complaints which can be raised before UN bodies if a NGO or government is prepared to present their case. However for the main part the general public has little direct contact with the UN and where it has, its role is purely passive.

The UN by itself can be differentiated from the UN System. The UN contains the General Assembly, the Security Council, the Economic and Social Council (ECOSOC) and its programmes and Secretariat led by the Secretary General. The UN has its own semi-autonomous agencies, such as the UN Environment Programme as well as direct responsibility for running its own technical cooperation programmes. There are also the wholly autonomous specialised agencies which report to the ECOSOC and cooperate in inter-agency work but have their own assemblies, governing bodies and budgets. Together they make up the UN System. The UN and the agencies for the main part close ranks when the System is under attack but will often contest fiercely their rights against each other. The System is diverse and polycentric; it is indeed a complex question whether such a situation produces more net costs or net benefits and for my answer, the reader must be persuaded to turn the pages.

INTRODUCTION

but have why to study attacks for future of UN

This book is written to assist in the process of
the reform of the United Nations (UN). The
criticisms of the UN have recently grown stronger,
going far beyond its detailed working, and
attacking the legitimacy that is the constitutional
basis of the institutions. If these attacks
continue, they will fundamentally undermine the UN
in much the same way as was the League of Nations
before the Second World War, finally destroying it.
     The kind of reform that could emerge from
either the gradual erosion of confidence in the UN,
or an economic or political catastrophe are not
acceptable solutions. The waste in experience in
global problem solving and rule setting would be
infinitely worse than with the League of Nations
because of the greater longevity, case experience
accumulated and width of problems covered. Reforms
are possible, but the complexities are very great,
not least because the criticisms of the UN stem
from a basic ambiguity. The UN is weak, but nation
states unwillingness to subordinate their national
interests to the good of the global commons
maintains it weak. Solutions must not only awaken
people to motivate reluctant governments, but also
satisfy some people's fears that global decision
making will not just suppress their local worries
in the interest of a mass global majority.
     Solutions are always easier on paper, however
sensitive the analysis and penetrating the answers.
Research and writing of books are not the only ways
to change the System. There are too many interests,
groups and levels with a stake in the result. No
one is going to take a blueprint in a book or a
research paper and translate it through some kind
of political machinery into an institutional
reality. The process itself is as important as the

1

rationale; both are equally balanced in the
moulding of the pressures of the moment which make
for a decision. The process of reforming the UN
will be an organic one with a life of its own and
the wider the net of the process is spread, the
more possible will it be to influence the
environment of the discussions.

Stage management can have an effect on the
outcome by providing succinct analysis, plausible
options, widening the process to open up new
options, as well as choice of timing to match an
economic upturn here, or a turn towards detente
there, to catch a possible political tide in the
favour of a more all-embracing reform.

Chapter 1 reiterates the essential rationale
for the UN looking as much to the future as to the
past, which strengthens the argument for reform
rather than outright abolition or continuous
attrition. Chapter 2 shows how minor existing
reforms have been and how the problems have been
evaded. It poses the questions about institutional
reform which are taken up in the separate studies
of Chapters 3-5. Chapter 2 makes the point that
separate studies of problems weakens the argument
for major institutional reform as there are common
institutional solutions for a number of problems.
Chapters 3-5 analyse the problem issues in depth to
isolate the common institutional solutions.
Chapter 6 is a conclusion in two ways. First, it
allows the author a little more scope for his own
judgement. Second, recommendations are made on what
at least the early stages of a 'Process of Reform'
might be so as to encourage ways in which the book
might be used and carried forward into a wider and
dynamic arena.

Chapter one

WHY THE UNITED NATIONS SYSTEM IS MORE THAN EVER
      NEEDED

The Charter objectives of the United Nations have
aged well after forty years:

> "WE THE PEOPLES OF THE UNITED NATIONS
> DETERMINED
>   to save succeeding generations from the
>   scourge of war, which twice in our life time
>   has brought untold sorrow to mankind, and
>   to reaffirm faith in fundamental human
>   rights, in the dignity and worth of the
>   human person, in the equal rights of men and
>   women and of nations large and small, and
>   to establish conditions under which justice
>   and respect for the obligations arising from
>   treaties and other sources of international
>   law can be maintained and to promote social
>   progress and better standards of life in
>   larger freedom "

Although these principles are as valid now as when
they were written, the world has grown more complex
and interdependent. There are in 1986 159 member
countries of the UN; when the Charter was signed in
1945, there were only 51. Different from 1945 are
some major influences.
    The world has changed since 1945; there has
been a dramatic rise in world trade and
communications of all sorts from telephone, telex,
computer link-ups and satellite television, to the
growth in personal air travel. The increasing
ability of money and credit to flow across national
boundaries inspite of governmental restrictions
has created a global capital market. International
labour migrations have transferred and juxtaposed
local cultures, unregarded in fast

rising economies but causing social stress when there is a recession. The movements of labour across international frontiers reflect the continuing disparities in levels of world living standards, especially with the poorest least developed countries and given the immense efforts that have gone into the promotion of development and the raising of expectations. Even more have expectations magnified in the once oil rich and middle income developing countries whose economies have grown significantly since 1945; these countries have been greatly affected by the recent recession, output and exports not being able to service the burden of debt incurred when there was an optimistic view of the future.

A counter trend to the increased global interdependence is the growing control on production and trade of fewer and larger economic entities, state agencies in the socialist East, trans-national corporations in the western market economies and sometimes link ups and arrangements between the two. Apart from the impact on the pattern of world investment, production and trade and the difficulty of adjusting development in the North to the competitive aspirations of the South, there is a real concern about the impact of this trend on the environment in the developing countries.

The strength of the trends leading to environmental degradation are daunting. The countries of the North, already industrialised, with relatively high standards of living, have great difficulty in accepting costly pollution control standards. The developing countries, trying hard and fast to industrialise, are very reluctant to put any pollution control brakes on their new industries. Trans-national corporations are able to transfer polluting industry to developing countries. It is an open question as to whether more environmental degradation is caused by industry seeking to reduce costs in highly competitive international markets or by the pressures of population growth and poverty. The land carrying capacity against rising population and industry has sometimes a higher threshold than that for the ecology. The world has many areas which have reached their ecological danger point, the foothills of the Himlayas, the Sahel, the Amazonian rain forest, the forests of northern Europe. Many countries are reaching the limit of their land carrying capacity; more than 40

4

developing countries are producing less grain per person in the 1980's than they did in the 1950's. There is concern about air and water pollution, the cutting down of woodlands and shrublands and overgrazing leading to soil erosion, soil salinity and alkinisation and increased water borne diseases from irrigation, the loss of flood restraining wetlands, genetic variety in plants and animals and the destruction of scenic beauty. In 1945 the environment was not a major issue; it is now.

The strength of the underlying economic trends have been so formidable partly because of the political rivalry of the nation states that inherited the world after 1945, limiting the capability to intervene effectively both to encourage development and to collectively preserve international peace and security. The failure to control the nuclear arms race in the early years after the second world war has bred a super power cold war. Within the shelter of the balance of mutual assured destruction, there have developed subtle forms of interstate aggression, economic and financial subversion, terrorism, clandestine or even overt support for guerilla forces, which can destabilise the government of a country and allow the superpowers to take part in and exacerbate conflicts anywhere in the world. Many of the developing countries that swelled the ranks of the original 51 members of the UN had fragile economic and political systems and were particularly susceptible to superpower destabilising influences.

All these influences make the problems faced by the UN in 1986 much more difficult than when it commenced its operations in 1945. Faced by such a formidable array of problems, is it really worth attempting to continue with the UN? Below, eight major rationales for the existence of the UN are posed, all of which suggest that outright abolition would be tragic and continued attrition, self defeating.

INSURE STATES AGAINST AGGRESSION

Ideological rivalry between Russia and the United States colours international relations in every corner of the globe; no country or regional alliance is immune. The conventional wisdom is that collective security could not be used against nuclear weapons states in the name of the United Nations without incurring nuclear retaliation

5

(Chapter 5 p.97). If the argument is taken at its face value, it would limit the value of Collective Security and indeed the argument must have some force, because the Charter powers (in Chapter VII) have rarely been invoked. However, Collective Security would still have a wide application to Third World countries and the Non-proliferation Treaty signatories. Also the conventional wisdom could be questioned; the possibility of using nuclear weapons at all as a military strategy is increasingly in doubt and superpowers, where they can, use mercenaries or 'local rebels' to fight their wars in preference to using their own troops. The value of Collective Security if it could be made functional for the Third World is reduction of superpower involvement in what otherwise would have been purely local conflicts.

Indirect aggression by subversion has grown in subtlety. Aid and military support both topple some governments and maintain others in power. Although economic sanctions are only effective under restrictive conditions, the increasing interdependence of trade and finance has widened the possibility of UN enforcement by non-military means. The same subtleties that are open to the aggressor would also be open to the UN, if the institutional capability of the organisation was widened.

PROTECT THE INDIVIDUAL AGAINST ABUSES OF HUMAN RIGHTS

Regional and national economic integration and technological change have put local economies and cultures under strain. One of the justified fears of encouraging trade and financial interdependence reinforced by a global organisation with universal values are that local interests and values could be eroded or submerged. A global organisation that did not deliberately recognise the conflict of interest and find an institutional counterbalance could never turn to a wider public audience for support, as that audience would be as distrustful of the UN as are their governments today. The UN has not and cannot just adopt a market response to all local values. It will be recognised that for example, the EEC philosophy is a purely market one, but in practice, for the agricultural sector, the EEC institutions are highly and perhaps overly protective. As concerns about religious groups, cultural minorities, waste of existing social infrastructure, environment degradation and cultural heritage, grow in national political importance, so will the UN have to find a place for a clearly rationalised check on some of its integration activities within its own institutional framework.

The UN recognises that states do not have the right to abuse their people but knows that such abuses are widespread and that there is no evidence of any decline of such abuses. The revolution in information and communication has only ensured that the technology of torture which has replaced the craft of torture has an unfortunate capability of being spread from one security force to another. Documentation of statistical evidence of mounting human rights violations is not available, only of the activities of human rights organisations so that at the moment, it has not been possible to quantify the numbers of human rights abuses and the trend over time.

Many Third World governments have new and fragile constitutions, shallow economic infrastructure, illogical boundaries, and with peoples divided by religion, tribe, or ethnic barriers. Unstable governments have sometimes preserved their power by quelling internal dissent up to and including torture and political murder. The UN can act as a forum for national and international human rights organisations as well as tighten the accepted codes of conduct and legal norms to check government abuses. However, there are limits to an intergovernmental UN where so many governments are guilty of human rights abuses and universal concensus is required for important decisions.

Problems of inter-country labour migration are on the increase. Labour migration is a manifestation of global interdependence, being encouraged when there were boom economic conditions and difficult to discourage when the global economy turns down. Similar pressures have further marginalised employment prospects of youth and women, the latter group made even more vulnerable as a result of localised long standing social customs. The more the principle of the UN protecting human rights and minority groups from government abuses is accepted, the greater will be the role of non-governmental organisations within the UN System. Also labour migration problems are another example where the UN will have to recognise the need to institutionalise, in some manner, a

brake upon over rapid economic integration. Without
those checks the UN will never retain the
allegiance of peoples as opposed to governments.
However, the problems are likely to be less in the
future as countries are much more wary of allowing
very rapid labour influx if boom conditions are
only likely to be temporary. Steady growth with
parallel rates of integration and labour migration
is not socially disruptive.

STEADYING AND REGULATING THE GLOBAL ECONOMY

Growing world trade and financial interdependency
between 1945 and 1980 have increased the demand for
global institutions to provide guiding rules, ease
the structural changes and loosen long standing
protectionist barriers. However, the persistent
recession since 1980 has set up a new pressure for
institutions that can regulate the global economy
and prevent a resurgence of protectionism.

The demand for the UN to coordinate and make
rules or laws to assist growing international trade
is still only a small part of many cross-national
institutional links that take place between
governmnents, private firms, national private
associations which represent those firms and
national non-governmental organisations, sometimes
grouped into international organisations. The UN
should only directly be involved where there are
especially difficult problems, not able to be
resolved by these groups, such as unstable basic
commodity prices, or where the groups may act in
ways inimical to the collective interest of
sufficient states for them to raise the issues in
the UN. For private or government agencies to raise
the issues in the UN, the institution has to be
capable of resolving them.

One indicator of the increased interaction in
the world economy is the way in which over the last
thirty years world trade has grown twice as much in
relation to the growth of world production. Table
1.1 taken from an UNCTAD Report illustrates the
variation in this relationship for OECD, US, Japan,
the socialist countries and the developing
countries.

Table 1.1

Share of Exports in GDP

(Percentage, based on data in current dollars)

Year	Developing Market Economy Countries				Socialist	Developing	World
	Total	OECD	US	Japan			
1950	10.1	9.9	4.5	9.8	..	12.8	10.6
1960	11.7	11.5	5.1	10.8	5.3	15.6	11.1
1970	13.7	13.5	5.7	10.8	5.8	15.9	12.5
1975	17.6	17.4	8.5	12.8	8.0	24.2	16.9
1980	20.6	20.2	10.2	14.0	8.9	26.8	19.6

Source: UNCTAD - "Trade and Development Report", 1984, 11.V. 23, page 54.

Increasing trade, is paralleled by the rise in personal travel, telecommunications and information transfer made available by cheaper and more efficient technology. Between 1951 and 1982, whereas the number of civil aviation kilometres flown increased about two times (from 1.6 billion to 3.5 billion), the number of passenger/kilometres increased (from 34.7 billion to 485.7 billion) nearly 14 times (that is passengers carried increased by 7 times).[1] The price of a transatlantic telephone call from London to New York fell by 75% in both of the 20 year periods from 1930-1950, as well as from 1950-1970, so that by 1970 it was at a level less than one-fifteenth of that 40 years previously.[2] Real time costing of computer mail communications is reducing costs further and will outdate and replace telex services. The economic benefits of interdependence will put pressure on the political will to accept it. There is political resistance to the speed and direction of change, both of which can be socially disruptive. Interdependency does not always imply gains for all parties, especially where one party (the South) is always one stage structurally and technologically behind (the North) and has more of an interest in commodities (with greater price and income elasticities) than manufactures.[3] The asymetrical dependency relationship is also important in arms aid and sales where there is a policy determined attempt to link the receiving country to the country giving or selling arms.[4] The UN becomes a forum for expressing some of the fears and disatisfaction at the growth of asymetrical interdependence.

Not all trends are asymetrical. There is a real bargain to be struck in the future between the South's growing manufacturing capacity and the North's service industries. The multi-dimensional political and economic bargaining that is involved in East/West trade is particularly suited to the UN Regional Economic Commission for Europe which has achieved research and dialogue but insufficient formal negotiating. In relation to the growth in North/South interdependency, there is still a long way to go in East/West trade.

In the future the relationship between the UN and transnational companies (TNC's) will need to become increasingly structured whereas at the moment there is tensioned ambivalence. The TNC's have many interests in common with the UN. Apart from the defence industry which has more significance in periods of global recession, the TNCs have a strong interest in peace. They, perhaps more than small firms and pressurised [5] individual marginal farmers, have the capability to take a long term time horizon to protect the environment. The question is can they be induced to use it? During the 1960-80 period, the top 200 companies (excluding socialist countries) increased their share of World GDP from 18 to 29%.[6] They have progressed from primary production, to processing and marketing developing country output. Global strategies soon result in flexible subsidiary location policies, a complex web of intrafirm trading across national boundaries, cross subsidising of product and services and hence the power to eliminate national competition. The TNCs have tended so far to be identified with the industrialised West, with individual countries where policies for the company may be set. The UN is composed of government representatives, some of whose members are at odds with TNC's. The heavy investment of the major banks in developing countries and TNCs has tended to focus on the need for global guidance and coordination to prevent a financial crisis. Floating exchange rates, the growth of the Eurodollar offshore currency market and rapid telecommunications have also reinforced the need for a global concensus. Currently, the major creditor countries are taking the lead and it is questionable at what point they will need to turn to the UN System institutions to provide more durable solutions to the linked problems.

RECTIFY GLOBAL INEQUALITIES

Global disparities of income are not much less sharp now than 40 years ago. Promoting social and economic development in developing and especially the least developed countries can remedy the great disparities of income and wealth between countries; so far efforts in this direction have not greatly reduced national income gaps. The question of rectifying global income gaps as an object of global policy stands apart from the issue of social and economic development and is considered separately here. As an object of UN policy, rectifying global income gaps is politically controversial.
        Redistribution within a country is politically somewhat less controversial than is international redistribution. Conservative influences in the

United States strongly object to the redistributive implications of the New International Economic Order (NIEO). These criticisms are finding their way through to government attack on the whole UN System.[7] Redistribution policies acknowledge the failure of "free market mechanisms" to correct imbalances[8] and those who are defending these mechanisms against 'socialist' ones are prepared to go to extremes.

Redistribution through taxation is less a socialist creed than social democratic philosophy. Socialists hold more that public control of institutions is necessary to effect real redistributive changes; taxation is too easily avoided. The NIEO contains some of both influences. The need for the UN on redistributive grounds rests a distinctly controversial objective but it is certainly one that will not go away, even on the threat of some of the richer nations to actually withdraw from the UN. The demands of some nations to withdraw from the UN can be likened to the demands of the Confederate States to withdraw from the Union in the US in 1864; the rich southern states were being asked to pay for the development of the north and they objected. Holding the UN together is at least as important today as maintaining the US Union was then; the solution however has to manifest itself in reasonable trade-offs in which all gain as the Brandt Reports[9] argue. However, it cannot be escaped that some struggles cannot be resolved by mutual degrees of surrender and gain and that a political battle is raging.

Until the institutions of the UN are stronger, it is unreasonable to make them stand the strain of major redistributive objectives. The UN should be the forum for political battles but not if they sunder the organisation. It is a fine line between submitting an institution like the UN to the necessary strains of real political battle and overstraining it so that its members begin to opt out. In a stable national government it is possible to change the political complexity of the government within its constitution; not so with the UN as it stands. If policies are not approved by one state, the other states of the UN cannot campaign for a new election or a realignment of parties within states, it can either tolerate the policy or leave the organisation. Redistribution is a fairer objective of the UN when the political battle ground is more adequately defined than it is at the present.

PRESERVE THE COMMON HERITAGE OF ALL MANKIND

The appreciation of global heritage is a relatively recent one and its awakening has come with the growth in communications. The pressures of population on limited land supply and the demands for a living by poor indigenous people place local cultural and environmental heritage at risk. Mankind has an interest in ensuring that not just purely local interests are consulted. The peoples of the world are increasingly willing to help the poorer countries cover the high costs of conservation of flora, fauna and areas of scientific, artistic or natural beauty; the UN to some extent must even anticipate this growth of public interest and concern, so that future generations do not regret the avoidable destruction of their joint patrimony.

SAFEGUARD THE INTERESTS OF FUTURE GENERATIONS

Traditional societies tend to safeguard their national resources; however, when population growth from migration and natural increase or natural disasters puts pressure on the existing population, then traditional patterns of conservation are overthrown. Economic competition and high interest rates put a premium on shortrun returns, whether it applies to feeding pattern of adults as against children in a drought stricken village, forest resource use in Nepal, Ivory Coast, and Brazil or bauxite mining in Papua New Guinea, reservoirs in Tasmania or chemical fertilizer intensive farming all over the world. National governments represent the long view against private short-term interests in their own countries but in many cases the global view has to be represented. The world of today can benefit from the innovation and dynamism of fast rising population growth, intensive use of natural resources, but the world of tomorrow could and most probably will suffer from climatic and soil deterioration and increasing proportion of marginal farm families. Nations will more and more want to delegate to the UN the irksome task of representing the next generations in the political dialogue and the UN will have to constantly remind governments of their responsibilities.

PROMOTE APPROPRIATE SOCIAL AND ECONOMIC DEVELOPMENT

The UN has seen the need for social and economic development from its first years but success has been elusive. There has been both development and growth in the poorer countries but in taking stock, the worries of population growth pressure on arable land, debt and payments deficits and low levels of absorbitive capacity have been increasing burdens. The base of development has to be broader to ensure its appropriateness; social acceptance of technologies through participation is required, more than technological transfer to the most modern sectors of the economy. These modern sector transfers will take place anyway; they can be guided to maximise local value added but they do not need to be promoted. Socially acceptable appropriate technologies for the rural and urban poor do need promotion and study because the pay off is slow and spread widely, giving rise to public as well as private benefits.

PEACEFUL RESOLUTION OF INTER-STATE DISPUTES

Peaceful settlement of disputes has been a constant international theme since the League of Nations and before. The need for acceptable procedures is even greater now because of the ideological war between the superpowers and their supporters and the exacerbation of disputes as a result of the intrusion of superpower issues. The peaceful settlement of a dispute between two or more states without some ultimate power of sanction if procedures are not kept is improbable. The number of disputes as such has probably not recently increased; it is only the power of escalation which has rendered some of them so dangerous to the global community. It would be less necessary to settle all disputes and probably easier to settle more of them if their global significance could be greatly reduced.

Notes to Chapter 1

1. UN - Statistical Yearbooks, 1951 and 1983.
2. S.J. Prais - "The Evolution of Giant Firms in Britain: a Study of the Growth of Concentration in Manufacturing Industry in

Britain 1909-1970", Cambridge, 1976. pp. 71 and 249.

3. UNCTAD documents have researched many of the fears of the South in economic and trade relationships in their conference documents and their Trade and Development Reviews. See for example, Review No. 5 of 1984 (E/F.84.II.D.8) "Changes in International Economic Relations in the Last Two Decades", pp 1-40. For a factual account, and Review No. 6 of 1985 (E.85.II.D.20), "Trade Links and dependency Theory", pp. 241-254 for bibliography.

4. C. Catrina - "Dependence and Interdependence in the Global Politico Military System" UNIDIR Research Paper No. 1, Geneva, 1985.

5. Traditional farmers tend to protect the environment, but major unusual pressures caused for example by a 'green revolution' or rapid population growth in relation to land supply overturns long term traditional values.

6. Clairmont F.F. and Cavanagh J.H. - "Transnational Corporations and Global Markets: Changing Power Relations", in UNCTAD Trade and Development Review, No. 4, Winter 1982 (E.83 II D.1), p.154.

7. Heritage Foundation (Editor Mr. B.Y. Pines) "A World Without A UN", Washington, D.C., 1984.

8. Sufficiently fast so that in the long run, as Keynes said, we are not all dead.

9. Independent Commission on International Development Issues - "North-South: a programme for Survival" Pan Books 1980. A Common Crisis: North-South Cooperation for World Recovery, Pan Books, 1983.

Chapter Two

REFORMING THE UN IS NOT EASY

PROBLEMS EXPAND, THE SYSTEM GROWS BUT CANNOT KEEP PACE

The UN System has responded to the growth in needs by setting up new agencies, IAEA (1957), IDA (1960), UNIDO (1966), IFAD (1976), Transnational Corporations (1974) are examples and not an exhaustive list. Each agency establishes some nearly autonomous programmes or units. UNEP's Regional Seas Programme, WHO's Expanded Programme of Immunisation, the Capital Development Fund of UNDP, the World Employment Programme of ILO, are examples. Bertrand[1] counted 20 distinct juridical elements for WHO, 18 for FAO, 10 for UNESCO and ILO, 15 for UN and 13 for UNDP, but he admitted that counting was difficult because there was only a fine line between a distinctly separate programme governed by an intergovernmental committee and one guided by a committee of experts which although nominally under the agencies own Committee and Council structure, is defacto autonomous.

The System has grown[2]; the problem is that each new agency is relatively short of funds for the role that it has been assigned; programmes are so all embracing that it is difficult to see the priorities and agencies duplicate activities without being able to programme an efficient coordinated effort. With the UN agency and programme or unit active at country level added to the presence of numerous bilateral and Non-governmental Organisations, it is little wonder that aid programmes overwhelm some governments. It is a major effort for UNDP to coordinate even if there was a will to cooperate. On the other side of

16

the argument it should be understood that
organisations working as far as possible from
central coordination has allowed target groups to
be reached which otherwise may have been blanketed
out by bureaucratic tangles or deliberate political
neglect.

The problems assumed by the agencies are
nearly always extremely difficult and are the very
areas where nation state governments and interest
groups have allotted the role to the UN because
they have failed to find solutions themselves. Each
of the needs expressed in chapter 1 are supported
by governments which may be willing in general
terms to countenance action in the area concerned,
partly in the knowledge that when their turn comes
for a direct approach by the agency to its problems
they will be taking a line representing their
national governments or interest groups. They
expect the agency to pursue the issues strongly,
but the agency has very limited powers to do so.

The UN and the agencies have provided a forum
for discussion of problems and have succeeded in
raising the level of awareness but when through
their technical cooperation programmes, they have
attempted to work with countries in making such
changes as are consistent with policies set, there
has been relatively little marked progress,
especially in areas where some significant private
or governmental interest is in conflict with the
policy or programme. The same conclusion applies to
the settlement of disputes; the UN has been able to
act as mediator but has not been allowed to
arbitrate without the agreement of the parties.
Peace-keeping forces are a considerable
achievement, but can only be put in place by
agreement of the parties and the absence of a
decisive dispute settlement procedure ensure they
will have to remain in position for an
indeterminate time, draining resources and patience.

The sectoral division of agencies work
conflicts with the inter-sectoral nature of
national developing country and even some of the
major inter-state developed country environment
problems.

"ce morcellement des activités n'est au
surplus compensé par aucune coordination
réelle ni sur le plan intellectuel ni sur le
plan méthodologique et institutionel. Chacune
des organisations a en effet non seulement ses
méthodes mais aussi sa doctrine sur le

17

> developpmement et sur les objectifs qui
> devraient être poursuivis par les pays
> receveurs.[3]

The sectoral UN agencies, World Health, Food and
Agriculture, Labour, Industry, link up with their
national ministry counterparts and reinforce the
lack of national coordination.

The recent innovation of world conferences on
major issues, such as environment, habitat, rural
development, have sponsored some bureaus or
agencies with relatively little finance or power to
effect coordination. Countries with special
interests or ideologies can finance and to some
extent control their special section of the UN.
National government funds parallel the allocation
of a high level post or posts in the agency or
sub-agency. The government of Japan has recently
made available additional funds for UN System
programmes and are confidently expected to raise
their contributions even higher. They are also at
the same time pressing for a significant number of
the expected vacant senior posts that will have to
be filled in the near future, including possibly
the Director General of UNESCO. In a System where
there is something for everybody priorities are set
by a kind of market place competition for funds and
national support.

There are those who may argue a UN System of
the market place is a sound philosophic concept.

> "On the national level, it is feasible and
> indeed desirable to have governmental units
> with clearly defined responsibilities. In this
> way uniform and coherent national policies can
> be formulated. But the world community is too
> heterogeneous, the sources of power too
> diffuse, and the problems too complex and
> varied for this approach to be workable. A
> pluralistic approach in which a diverse set of
> organisations, servicing different clienteles,
> attempts to deal with complex and multifaceted
> problems is perhaps a better one. Moreover the
> confusion that results from two or more
> organisations attempting to deal with the same
> set of problems can be counter-balanced by the
> gains that result from the competition
> injected into the system".[4]

The problem is that an organisation which aims
to accomplish and not just to discuss, to focus on

long term and not just expedient short-term goals
and to make law and policy in areas of collective
but possibly not individual state interests, cannot
operate with such a philosophy. Recognising that
they are not having much success in the most
difficult areas of global priority, some agencies
have accepted remedial short-term goals which may
in the long run create at least as many problems as
they solve.

There is not only competition for funds
between agencies but competition in philosophy.This
does not confuse most countries because it is a
mirror image of their own plurality, but it does
not guide them in avoiding errors; for example, the
environmental problems of large scale industry,
irrigation schemes, the employment impact of
subsidised labour displacing technology, might have
been avoided if there was a common policy and joint
programmes. It can be argued that no agency has a
monopoly on successful programming; no one knows
the answers and plurality may produce more of them.
A reply is that it is a costly way to find answers
and over forty years has not itself succeeded in
producing them.

A HISTORY OF MINOR REFORMS

Many reforms accommodate the expansions to the
System so that reform is more apparent than real.
More far reaching reforms may not have required so
many and dispersed additions to the System. There
has been only one major effort to actually
restructure the System. This took place between
1974 and 1979. The pressure for reform came from
the North; they were looking for major improvements
in UN efficiency. The timing coincided with the
drive for a New International Economic Order and a
resurgence of confidence on the part of the South
as a result of the rise in oil prices and the
effort to achieve reform took four years and even
then, as is recounted later, the outcome (known as
the Dadzie reforms,see page 19) was disappointing.
The South had not been offered the bargain for
reform they were seeking, which was a major
conference on 'global North/South negotiations'.

Apart from additions to the UN itself and
specialised agencies (of which there has been one,
IFAD), reforms fall into three groups. The first
group attempts to accommodate the rising tide of
new developing country membership. Second, is the

acknowledgement by the representative organs of the System that they must bring about more inter-unit and agency coordination. Third, is the group of measures and attempted measures to improve peaceful settlement of disputes procedures, especially the effectiveness of the Security Council.

Reforms Arising from the Arrival of the Developing Countries in the UN

The enlargement of the Security Council from 11-15 members in 1966 falls into the first group. The Jackson reforms[5] of 1970-71 also come into the first group. These reforms allowed the funds in the UNDP to be programmed according to national developing country determined priorities rather than a country allocation of an agreed agency share of a global total - a sensible decision when agency policies are not coordinated around an agreed inter-agency global strategy, but makes less sense if ever such a strategy can be devised and sustained. Into this group also come the attempts to set up a major combined technical assistance and funding agency (SUNFED)[6] and a combined trade organisation (ITO)[7] which would have fulfilled the functions of both GATT and UNCTAD.At the time of the struggles to establish these more comprehensive organisations, the developing countries were too weak in number and economic power for the developed countries to consider that it was even worth establishing such negotiating forums. By the time that the developing countries had gained power because of their increase in numbers, their economic growth, and from the weight added by their OPEC members in the 1975-80 relative high oil price period, the developed countries were not interested. They had become too concerned about the possible outcome of such negotiations to encourage any profound restructuring of the institutions of negotiation, although they had been pressing for internal UN efficiency and coordination reforms, not at all the same thing as will be appreciated.

Reforms to Improve Coordination

The group of reforms clustered around the motivation of improving coordination of the gradually increasing number of UN System units, sub-units and specialised agencies has gathered only slow momentum. The power of Secretariat hirearchy over lower echelons or semi-autonomous units and agencies is very limited, more because of the relationship these units build up with sectoral or area constituencies for extra budgetary funds or representative support, than for any want of Secretariat budgetary or disciplinary control. So tied in are many representatives on the various controlling bodies of each unit, organisation and agency that the need for reform is given second priority to not disturbing these strong proprietary mutually supporting relationships. This stricture applies to control not only by the General Assembly over agencies but also, any agency over its semi-autonomous programme or unit. The really important deficiency is in inter-agency coordination. It is only when the need becomes blatant and overwhelming that in the higher level bodies like the General Assembly, or its Committees, binding inter-agency decisions can be taken. This partly explains why the reform initiatives have only been very ad hoc, even in the period 1975-80 when the developing country majority and power in the General Assembly was at its height.

Three examples can be given of reforms to produce greater efficiency and coordination. First the General Assembly instituted special sessions to deal with urgent political problems and after 1974 the meetings were used to discuss major inter-sectoral issues where important decisions were sought. Second, a series of worldwide expert conferences with much NGO preparation were instituted also on inter-sectoral issues, starting in 1972 with the UN Conference on the Human Environment in Stockholm, to provide a globally acceptable concensus and recommendations for the General Assembly. Other examples are the conferences on population 1974 and 1984, Women's conference 1975, HABITAT 1976, Water 1977, Desertification 1977, Technical Cooperation among developing countries 1978, Primary Health Care 1978, Agrarian Reform and Rural Development 1979. The third attempts to produce improved coordination were in the "Dadzie Reforms" of 1977, named after the Chairman of the Ad hoc Committee on the restructuring of the UN Economic and Social Sectors which recommended them. These reforms took a long time to produce and were less than profound, partly because the developed countries were not prepared to accept that global negotiations on a New International Economic Order was a fair trade off for the developing country acceptance of the reform

package. The Dadzie reforms effectively introduced
a Director-General of a Department of Development
and streamlined and ordered the work of the
inter-agency Advisory Committee on Coordination
(ACC). The report [8] of the Ad-hoc Committee
chaired by Ambassador Dadzie recommended more far
reaching reforms than were introduced and the
Expert report that was an input to the Dadzie
Committee had even more radical proposals.[9] The
General Assembly resolution 32/197 embodied the
recommendations of the Dadzie Committee but the
weakness of General Assembly resolutions is
illustrated by the levels of response to the many
recommendations, even from the semi-independent
agencies within the UN System (studied in Chapter
4). For the main part the Dadzie report accepted
the sectoral division of related and specialised
agencies.

Reforms Responding to the Blockages in the Security Council

Agreements were arrived at early in the history of
the UN that certain votes in the Security Council
could be taken as a question of procedure and hence
without the veto[10] and that an abstained vote was
not a negative vote or veto. The motivation was the
Security Council's practical operational
efficiency. The real issues such as the substantive
responsibilities of the Security Council in peace
and security remained subject to the veto of the
five permanent members (USSR, US, Great Britain,
France and China).
    One device was found for escaping the veto,
the Uniting for Peace Resolution[11]. The Security
Council on a procedural vote passes a peace and
security matter to the General Assembly because it
is unable to resolve the question itself. The
General Assembly can then deal with the question
under its voting procedures. This device has been
used to the discomfiture of both superpowers since
its introduction in 1954 but its unpopularity and
possible illegality has inhibited further
development (studied further in Chapter 5).
    The greater participation of the developing
country members in the Security Council, reflecting
their increasing importance in world politics, has
probably emphasised the negative role of the veto.
In 1966 the number of members was increased from 11
to 15 and the number of affirmative votes required
for a positive decision from 7 to 9. The developing

countries maintain a disciplined block vote of nine, but because of the potential veto of the permanent members, this block vote can only be used to prevent a decision rather than enforce one. The gradual acceptance of non-voting parties to a dispute being present at debates also has widened developing country participation unmatched by any additional power to influence final decisions.

The question of the increasing role of block meetings and private consultations before Security Council meetings is less clear cut; caucas meetings can increase the element of secret diplomacy which is necessary to solve complex problems but can turn plenary sessions into declarations of posture rather than real debate. The caucas meetings and negotiations do produce the kind of horse trading found in most political systems where representatives are distanced from their voting public, but if at the end of the private sessions more positive decisions were possible, the caucas system could allow a workable process of peaceful disputes settlement to gain foundation. There would then be, as there is not now, a reasonable balance between private caucas meetings and open sessions with votes taken.

ESCAPING FROM THE DILEMMA OF ATTAINABLE AND IRRELEVANT OR RADICAL BUT UNATTAINABLE REFORMS

Suggestions for reform of the UN are numerous covering both social and economic institutions as well as those responsible for peace and security. They divide rather easily into those which might be acceptable or more likely, have already been accepted for example, as a result of the Dadzie reforms, but have not changed the fundamental problems and those more radical reforms where the political stumbling blocks are daunting.

If irrelevant reforms are rejected, however attainable, then what are the political stumbling blocks which are so formidable.

The Institutionalisation of the Power of National Sovereignty

The Charter of the UN places all responsibility on to member states. The organisation only has powers to enforce through the Security Council if there is a breach of security. The veto and the cold war has effectively prevented its use. In all other respects states can refuse to cooperate and the UN

cannot reply except with weapons that can be
ignored. Resolutions in the General Assembly which
are not unanimous are now virtually disregarded.
Dialogue and discussions can take place on
important issues but as there is always the
possibility of refusal, many important decisions
are avoided. States can vote against resolutions
and not sign treaties based on them or even vote
for and still not sign. Signed treaties are usually
kept although there are frequently legal
loopholes; accepting treaties is one step but
applying them is another. Even where there are
systems of verification and supervision of the
application of treaties as in the case of the ILO's
supervision machinery for labour Conventions, the
IAEA's 'Safeguards' procedure to ensure Nuclear
Non-proliferation Treaty signatories use nuclear
power plant, equipment and supplies only for
peaceful purposes and the human rights supervision
procedures for treaties (torture, racial
discrimination for example), there are loopholes.
The fact that there is one ILO unified process of
supervision for labour Conventions is a major
strength but the Committee of Experts that
undertakes most of the technical work comments on
1200 cases per year and reports that there is
progress on a mere 41 of them(in 1985[12]; the
average per year between 1974 and 1983[13] was 76.
For human rights there are nearly as many
supervision procedures, commissions and Secretariat
units as there are treaties. Treaty supervision
procedures are only accepted by states when there
is a really strongly perceived need and no
alternative.
    Some UN agencies are strongly supported by a
few states with voluntary funding contributions
whilst others pay nothing. For example the budget
of UNDP comes almost entirely from voluntary
pledges. Pledges in 1984 amounted to $674.9 million
and seven countries contributed $447.2 million or
66.3% (US, Japan, Canada, Norway, Sweden,
Netherlands, and the Federal Republic of
Germany).The top six countries by their per-capita
contributions are Norway($11.66), Denmark($8.28),
Sweden($5.89), Netherlands($3.41),
Switzerland($2.86) and Canada($2.10). For the
biennium 1984/85, the Advisory Committee on
Coordination [14]of the UN estimated that total
System expenditure would be $11.1 billion of which
$7.4 billion would be funded from extra budgetary
sources, that is outside the regular budget (of

which the UNDP figure of about $1.3 billion will be included). This discretionary funding gives the major western donors considerable influence over the programmes and even over whole agencies and though it greatly augments the funds of the agencies, it creates tension in the agency assemblies where budgets are debated and priorities are layed down.

The argument that the unacceptable alternative is an all powerful supranational body is only valid because states are sovereign, that is they are unlikely to vote for the safeguards which would make a supranational body a valid alternative. These safeguards are to have direct or even indirect elections for some kind of global policy making Cabinet and to give a share of the decision making powers to a functional parliament modelled for example, somewhat on ILO's tripartite assembly. In weighing up the practical from the purely theoretical solutions, it should be remembered that the European Parliament at Strasbourg owed its origins to being incorporated in a sectoral agency, the European Coal and Steel Community,first with only six members and grew by transference to a wider responsibility and more countries.[15] It now has directly elected MP's, virtually powerless but a reality which can only grow in status.

It Will be Difficult to Reform the Charter

The Charter was amended to increase the number of members of the Economic and Social Council and the Security Council[16] but these changes are innocuous relative to the major changes required. The Charter can be amended by two procedures but with similar onerous voting constraints. The first under Article 108 requires a two-thirds majority of the General Assembly and by a vote of any nine members of the Security Council, including all the permanent members. The second under Article 109 allows for a General Conference; any changes recommended by a two-thirds vote of the Conference must then be ratified by two-thirds of the member states including all the permanent members of the Security Council. Thus, the permanent members of the Security Council can veto any constitutional change.

The Agencies Have an Interest in the Status-quo.

The specialised agency secretariats prefer their autonomy even at the expense of (what some of them believe to be a spurious) increase in efficiency. The United Nations Development Programme Resident Representatives and Coordinators (RRUNDP's), responsible for coordination at the country level, frequently have a hard time eliminating duplication and aligning the timing of what could be complementary agency programmes. The UNDP Administrator himself admits this:

> "In some instances, while recognising the desirability and necessity of direct links beween agencies and sectoral ministeries, Resident Coordinators may nonetheless face difficulties in ensuring that the consultation process among country representatives of the UN system maintains the desired level of co-ordination of United Nations technical co-operation activities."[17]

Agency governing bodies hardly, if ever, hold joint meetings; such meetings might have reinforced the existing System coordination machinery (described in chapter 4), which is insufficiently powerful to enforce coordination.[18] Agency secretariats use their power of patronage to maintain their positions.

> "Les pouvoirs dictatoriaux dont il (the Directors General) dispose en matiere de personnel et de recruitment accroissent encore ses possibilites d'influence"[19]

Hence the complaints of secretariat staff associations,supported by statistics from the ACC Consultative Committee on Administrative and Budgetary Questions, that it is difficult to obtain internal promotion and that there are far too many unneccessary new appointments from outside the agency.

> "in many cases the organisations attract proportionately more 'fresh blood' at the highest level(D-2 Grade) than at the P.5 level. This may be due in some cases to the interest of the member states in the appointment of senior staffs."[20]

Chapter 4 studies the issue of rural development as one of the areas where inter agency joint planning and programming is required. Evidence from the many reviews of the United Nations Joint Inspection Unit on the subject of agency coordination and planning are cited to illustrate the point as well as specific references to the difficulties under which the inter-agency coordination committee for the International Drinking Water and Sanitation Decade(1981-1990) is labouring and how small have been the results of its efforts. In addition Maurice Bertrand, the now retired Inspector from the Joint Inspection Unit (JIU) in his report advocating the reform of the United Nations, already quoted, sees the eventual abolition of the sector agencies as the only way to overcome the problems arising from agency autonomy.

Only in a Period of Detente can Progress be Made

A country's political standpoint may greatly influence its attitude towards cooperation with the UN and UN reform. Sam Cole in a study for UNITAR[21] put forward three futures scenarios which illustrate the fundamentally different ideologies and global objectives of certain governments. The conservative view corresponds to a highly competitive society where there are only minimal needs for international cooperation. The radical view also considers that there is little point in cooperation from the standpoint of the East and South and that the South should de-link from the North which is only an economic and political burden. Only with the third reformist viewpoint which mixes East/West detente and a New International Economic Order between North and South can there be significant progress towards international cooperation and hence UN reform. With some signs of a powerful trend towards detente in the socialist East but with the elections in the North West producing widely differing governments between their ideological viewpoints, what are the chances a converging towards a reformist position sufficient to generate the desired structural changes in the UN? Only the diminishing number of military dictatorships in the South gives real cause for optimism.
    The process of creating a peaceful settlement of disputes procedure is burdened with difficulties:

27

Reforming the UN is not Easy

(i)   Superpower conflict heightens short term
        political problems. Each superpower rivals
        for influence in the Third World not only to
        enhance prestige or its view of political
        philosophy, but for the very much more
        important reasons of global economics and
        military security; markets, secure
        investments and military bases are the
        dominant motives. These influences are
        overlaid on the governments of the Third
        World who are fragile economically and
        politically and vulnerable to threats on
        their immediate frontiers. In the absence of
        a UN collective security guarantee, many
        Third World and non-aligned countries look
        to the superpowers for economic aid in hard
        times as well as military security. However
        they are becoming increasingly more
        sceptical after the major setbacks by the
        U.S. in Vietnam and by the USSR in
        Afghanistan. Countries that are under severe
        threat from one superpower have very little
        alternative but to turn to the other,
        especially if economic blockades or covert
        subversion are undermining the security of
        the state. How long can a government
        continue to withold making requests for
        assistance to one superpower in order not to
        justify the accusation from the other that
        it should be brought down because it has so
        asked for help? The case of Nicaragua
        approximates very closely to this scenario.

(ii)   The trade-off between less Third World
        influence in the General Assembly for
        reduced permanent member control over the
        Security Council is not clear to either
        block, so neither is willing to sacrifice
        their current strengths for a more nebulous
        and long term benefit.

(iii)   In this period of great stress between the
        major power blocks, each takes a pessimistic
        view, even if it is sometimes contradictory
        (the US regards the Third World as tending
        towards socialism and against free
        enterprise; the USSR needs constantly to woo
        the Third World which is predominantly mixed
        market economies to prevent the socialist
        vote being swamped); the Third World
        considers the superpowers use nuclear arms
        as a means to enhance their economic and

military superiority and Third World
dependence.

Many Governments and the Secretary-General of the UN Have at Most a Medium Term Time Horizon

Transnational issues tend to be long-term; natural
resource development, the environment, health,
population issues, racial and cultural harmony,
human rights, all are problems where investment in
effort and capital has a long gestation period.
Investment in the UN System has probably a ten year
plus gestation period. Governments with elections
in a few years or governments with oppositions
fomenting rebellion have a shorter time horizon.
Even a Secretary-General of the UN who seeks a
second term cannot afford to alienate key votes if
he wishes to be re-elected.

Many People and Powerful Interest Groups May Take a More Localised or Conservative View than Their Governments on Global Issues

Nowhere has the message been widely received that a
reform of the UN which strengthened central policy
direction, settled disputes peacefully and made
binding international law, would also preserve
cultural diversity and local economic development.
Many peoples would react negatively to a
strengthening of the UN and centralised policy
direction as have national regions, and sectoral
interests in the European Economic Community; the
stronger UN might imply the economic decline of
their national region or their industry. In a
global or world region recession, national
interests grow stronger and governments are
probably under-representing the views of some of
their most powerful interest groups.
    To escape from the horns of the dilemma of
trivial attainable or radical unrealistic reforms,
I recommend bending one of the two horns, a radical
reform with a realistic possibility. To make the
reform realistic, a process has to be devised which
takes into account the formidable blockages to
progress listed above. The process chosen must be
itself a political force and the reforms
recommended have to be sufficient to defuse a large
area of the opposition. Catching the tide of
economic and political affairs is also important.
As Karl Marx preached, the economic forces are very
important and to work with them can bring a much

29

greater chance of success. However, there is no
inevitable march of these forces; they do not all
work in the same direction. For example, global
recession in the 1980's breeds protectionism and
strong national and sectoral stands on issues, but
it also causes international financial and
political crises which develops a pressure for
global solutions. Measuring the net strength of
these important trends and timing the actions taken
in the process of reform is crucial.

A PROCESS WHICH CAN RAISE THE CEILING OF REFORM
OBJECTIVES

Only partially is the process chosen independent of
the reform outcomes. It is not necessary and
probably politically very unwise to try and
prejudge the issues and present a limited set of
proposals to the international community, however
comprehensive and inter-related. To a large extent
the process has to be allowed to develop its own
momentum and make its own decisions. It is a major
objective in itself to establish a really broad
based process of reform which has its own momentum.
Nevertheless a major role for people's
participation, NGO's, the Regional Commissions in
the process carries important implications for the
directions which will be taken by the reforms
proposed. If the reform outcomes are likely only to
involve member states, then it is not only unwise
to aim to open the·process up so widely, it is not
feasible.
      A more certain and weighty process has to be
assured before it is possible to be ambitious for
the reform outcomes. Are there any process
innovations which give ground for optimism? Some
general principles about the process should be
agreed first:

The Widest Ranging Debate Consistent with Time
Available.Although it would have been ideal to have
reform proposals ready within two years to catch
the pressure of economic crisis and any political
detente, the absolute minimum for a major global
debate is five years.

Reform Objectives Should be Staggered.Instead of
regarding the Charter of the UN as immutably fixed
for all time, some long term objectives should be
set with which the more immediately attainable

30

medium term and short term objectives should be consistent. The process of reform should be such that it can encompass all three groups of objectives.

The Details of the Process of Reform Should be Rolled Forward. If the process of reform included annual steps, then only the next and the one after should be worked out in detail; the details for the future steps should be agreed when the reform proposals and options become clearer with each succeeding step.

The Headings of a Process Should be Agreed as a First Step. The process chosen will be debated long and hard and each step will be perused by the major blocks for any ideological or significant socio, religious or cultural bias. The issue of the size and shape of the table must be taken seriously, the process for agreeing 'the process'. The debate on the process could best take place in the General Assembly and Security Council as part of the negotiations on the initiating resolution. The major issue is whether both superpowers will agree each others suggestions for organisations that should participate in each stage of the debate and the political balance of any country groupings that composite the recommendations for a General Conference to absorb. The last two steps of the process could be a General Conference and the ratification procedures under Article 109 of the Charter. The immediate or even medium term recommendations may not require Charter revision so that the General Conference may not need to invoke Article 109 unless it was necessary and final ratification was feasible.

How Much Compromise to Preserve Universality

One or two powerful countries could hold up a concensus beyond the point where it may be regarded as reasonable. It may be rational from the short term self interested point of view of those countries, but against the common interest of a broad spectrum of other member countries. What then? To go forward would risk losing the country or countries from the Organisation which would be nothing less than a tragedy. Nevertheless, a reformed organisation of 157 rather than 159 member countries may be preferable, however much economically and politically weakened. The gain

from reforms for states who remain members may
balance the loss of funds and the ending of
universal membership. The cost of universality may
be too high and this issue should itself be part of
the debate.

A possible outline process for reform is
indicated in the concluding chapter 6. In all
events the hinge point in the process is a General
Conference which can initiate, but not finalise
Charter reforms. The most important issues are to
ensure that packages of reforms are produced for
the General Conference which balance the great
forces of North/South, East/West and which if they
imply Charter reform, have the support of the
permanent members enough to allow the final step of
reform ratification.

COMMON INSTITUTIONAL SOLUTIONS LINKING THE MAJOR
GLOBAL ISSUES

Despite the proliferation of agencies and bodies of
the UN System, there are relatively few nominal
controlling structures at the peak of the System;
there are the General Assembly, the Security
Council and the Economic and Social Council. Below
them, the assemblies and governing bodies of the
specialised agencies or councils and other
committees which run sub-structure or major
programmes have various degrees of autonomy.

The problem is that there is very little real
control in the System.

There is No Resolution of the Balance of Voting in the System to Allow Effective Control

There are all kinds of voting structures in the
organs of the System which satisfy some members but
not others and to such an extent that the opposing
countries prefer to take their international
problem solving elsewhere for solution. There is
nothing basically wrong with the principle of
different voting structures for organisations that
have different purposes; the voting structure for
human rights issues, which spends little money,
need not be weighted more towards the developed
countries as say for the World Bank which is
funding development with mainly developed country
derived resources. The issue is however much deeper
if the Charter bodies themselves, specifically the
General Assembly and the Economic and Social
Council, which should guide and control the System,

do not have a voting structure which has the basic
confidence of all the essential participating
members. Without control, the System agencies,
sub-agencies and programmes proliferate, refuse to
be coordinated, devise separate and sometimes
inconsistent policies, fragment and duplicate their
efforts and dissipate their scarce resources on
high overhead secretariat costs.

Insufficient Committment to Issues and System Structure Make for a Conservative Response to Programme Financing

A study [22] made in the early 1960's of United
Nations financing came to the conclusion that the
constant trend in UN financing was that it has
always been in a crisis situation. A comparison
made with other intergovernmental organisations and
other parts of the UN System showed that coherence
around the objectives of any international
organisation made for consistent support for its
financing and a diffuse set of issues and loyalties
overspilled on to the willingness to support the
budget.

> "..the quest for technical formulae in the
> absence of polical concensus may be an
> exercise in futility".[23]

The size of the contribution to the UN budget for
most countries is such an insignificant sum in
their own budgets, that without the political
significance of the payments, one wonders what all
the fuss is about. Even at the time of the study,
in 1964, no state contributed as much as one half
of one percent of its GNP. The contributions of 78
states fell between .005 and .035 per cent. Because
the 1964 study is some what dated, it is worth
confirming that the situation in 1986 is
fundamentally the same. The table below shows the
top ten contributors to the regular budget of the
UN for 1985[24], the percentage assessment
(proportion of the UN budget),and the percentage
each contribution makes to their own GNP.

Reforming the UN is not Easy

Table 2.1
    The Top Ten Contributors to the UN
        1985 Regular Budget

country	% UN assessed	contribution $ Mil.	% of GNP
United States	25.0	197.9	.006
USSR	10.4	69.4	.010
Japan	9.8	67.9	.006
Germany FRG	8.1	56.2	.008
France	6.5	42.8	.008
UK	4.7	30.7	.006
Italy	3.7	24.6	.007
Canada	3.1	20.3	.007
Spain	3.2	17.7	.007
Netherlands	1.8	11.7	.008
Sweden	1.3	8.7	.006
total above		547.9	
total Budget		691.9	

The study also demonstrated that from the
UN's earliest days a relatively few developed
countries from the North and West paid a very high
proportion of the assessed budget. This is clearly
as true in 1985 as it was in 1964. Also it is
confirmed how insignificant the UN regular budget
is as a cost burden on the countries who pay the
most.

The first assessments were made on the basis
of Gross National Product(GNP), GNP per capita and
war damage and the result for the United States
was that it ended up assessed to pay nearly 40% of
the regular budget of the organisation. Gradually
this was reduced, in the 10 years after 1946 to
30% and then to the current assessment of 25% of
the budget; the United States has only been
maintaining the complaint that it has been making
since the organisation was started. The assessment
is now based only on GNP and per capita GNP(that
is GNP and population); there is also an agreed
principle which says that no one country should
pay more than 30% or less than .04% of the total
budget and the members have so far resisted further
changes in the criteria. Very similar percentage
assessments are made for the regular budgets of all
the specialised agencies. It should be remembered
that the developed countries are willing to cover
over 60% of the total System budget with voluntary
contributions. The issue is less the method of
assessment but that the developed countries are

unwilling to allow the monies completely out of
their control. With a high proportion of voluntary
funds, they have many more ways of controlling how
the funds are used, from approval of the programmes
for which the funds are intended to regular
programme reviews. Unhappiness with the way votes
and control have moved to the South has
strengthened the resistance of the developed North
and West to all the regular budgets of the System
and only by implication to the UN whose budget is
more dependant on the regular assessment.

The socialist block has also taken a long
-standing position on the financing of
peace-keeping forces which have been the largest
expenditures of the UN. They have not in general
been in favour of peace-keeping and have refused to
make any blanket commitment to pay for the UN
peace-keeping exercises. The issue that
peace-keeping was a legitimate expenditure for the
UN proportionate assessment was taken to the
International Court of Justice(ICJ) for an Advisory
Opinion.[25] Despite the ICJ's 1962 ruling that
they were a legitimate expense, on a majority vote,
peace-keeping forces have only been financed as a
result of a tacit agreement to use a special
assessment excluding the developing countries.
However cumulative witholdings from the special
assessments for Cyprus(UNEF) and the Syria observer
forces(UNDOF) amount to $30.9 million and $209.5
million for the Lebanon force(UNIFIL) (by September
1985). In practice the funding has been
disproportionately borne by the troop donating
countries. Hence any country which allocates forces
for peace-keeping knows that it will be carrying
most of the costs for its contribution.

The general indiscipline by the broad
membership of the UN to making regular payments and
correcting arrears of payments adds to the long
-standing and growing financial crisis. As at the
30th June 1985, only 33 member states of the UN or
less than 21% of total members had paid their 1985
assessed contributions to the regular budget in
full, 26 countries had made partial payments, 29
had not paid but were not in arrears and as many as
71 were both in arrears and had not paid the 1985
contribution. The situation in 1986 has grown
worse; all temporary expedients open to the
Secretary General having been exhausted and with
much of the strain having to be borne quite
unfairly by the Secretariat. By the end of 1985 the
accumulated deficit on the regular budget had

reached $116.3 million and $390.7 million for the peace-keeping account. The forecast 1986 cash flow position had become critical because of the expected withholding by the US of some $55 million of its UN assessment plus expected effects from depreciation of the dollar, costing an additional $30 millions. If other states also were late or withheld contributions, the forecast cash shortfall could go over $100 million. All the working capital and reserves had been eaten up to cover past arrears. The Secretary General was led to ask for a Special Session of the General Assembly on the issue but nobody expects anything but short term expedient solutions[26].

The position of the specialised agencies is not dissimilar; at the 30th September 1985, there was $389 million outstanding as a result of unpaid contributions for all the agencies[27]. There is no question that if anything more than another temporary solution to the financial crisis is to be found, it will require some more permanent solutions to the structure of the whole UN System. The 1986 decision of the United States to reduce its contribution from 25 to 20% has only brought the crisis to a head.

Technical Complexity Requires Either Effective Methods of Coordination or Decentralization

The large variety of problems dealt with by the UN System and the tight sectoral division of the agencies and frequently the programmes demand coordination and control. There are basically two types of solution:

(a) centralised planning and managerial control
(b) geographical or regional decentralisaton.

The System will choose the first if it is forced to accept greater coordination and control because it preserves the sectoral agencies. The second would replace the sector agencies in a radical reform by stronger regional commissions or agencies. However, it should be appreciated that if the decentralisation is not to amount to total 'devolution' of all responsibility, then there will still be a need to devise and control the regional agencies at the policy level (including managerial evaluation and discipline). That implies that control is required in both cases, the one using the existing sector agencies, the other reforming

the agencies from sectors to regions. What we must
ask is, if planning and policy direction are still
required for regional agencies, is the regional
reform likely to produce such improvements of
coordination to justify the major upheaval involved
in abolition of the sector agencies?

Temporary and Medium Level Political Country Representatives Cannot Control the Secretariats of the UN and Agencies

The question is raised whether it is necessary to
introduce a third type of agent in the UN System
framework. At the moment there is the Secretariat,
responsible to the Secretary General and the
country representatives, usually civil servants
from the sectoral ministries who attend the
Assemblies and Executive Bodies of agencies. These
representatives are frequently middle level civil
servants, as sectorally separated as the agencies
they attend, frequently insufficiently briefed
before they come, and temporary both as regards the
brevity of the meetings and to the rotation of
representatives in successive meetings. The
European Community has national Commissioners who
run a specific part of the EEC Secretariat.
Although they are part national representative and
part secretariat, their responsibliity is to the
President of the Commission and all their officers
report to them and not to a Secretary General. What
would be required in the UN is some way that the
Executive Boards of the agencies and the General
Assembly of the UN can delegate broad
responsibilities to Commissioners who can act
either together as a group or individually for
their own area. Their main use would be in inter
agency coordination and for specific and temporary
tasks; if more was required of them, the question
could be legitimately raised why not simply
strengthen the executive boards of agencies or the
Secretariat. One answer is that the General
Assembly has no executive board and its Committees
suffer from all the same problems as regards
country representatives as does the plenary
Assembly. The members of executive boards of UN
agencies are national government representatives
themselves whereas Commissioners would be paid
officers of the agency. In addition the Security
Council, which is a second autonomous body, not
really holding itself responsible to the General
Assembly, has the veto rule as a major structural

limitation. The advantage of Commissioners are that they are a degree more technical than representatives and because of their four year term of office on appointment from the Council, a degree more political than the Secretariat.

The arguments against using Commissioners in the agencies as well as selectively in the UN itself are still very weighty. Commissioners would tend to undermine the power of both the secretariat, as well as the executive boards. The oil and water not mixing analogy describes this problem; either the model of the assembly, board and secretariat is adhered to, or there must be a radical adoption of the system used by the EEC of a Council of Ministers and Commissioners. It is not easy to see how the mixture might work and even within the UN, its use could only be very selective if it was not to erode the responsibility of the Secretariat and the Committees. If a UN Under-Secretary General had been given the same delegated powers as a EEC Commissioner, he too might be able to carry out his functions effectively. It would be advisable that if commissioners are to be used in the UN System, maintaining the structure broadly as it is now, they should be used very sparingly.

The Agencies Have Major Types of Activity in Common

The fact that for instance three agencies such as ILO, UNCTAD and UN Human Rights Commission inter-alia may need to negotiate and perhaps supervise agreements, conventions or treaties between countries does not imply amalgamation or even coordination. What it does imply is that the functions be recognised where they are neglected, that the methods used be cross analysed by agencies and where useful, solutions are incorporated by other agencies. The work of the UN and the agencies covers five tasks:

1. Problem analysis and policy prescription for problems common to a large number of countries;
2. Agency long and medium term planning and programming of their budgets for expenditure, especially at country level;
3. Arranging negotiations between countries (peaceful settlement of disputes, treaties, conventions and agreements making covering

nearly all the areas of responsibility of the
UN System);
4. Standard setting, international law making,
compliance verification and treaty supervision;
5. Public education, communication, information
and participation in UN affairs.

Taking as an example the problem of development,
agencies such as WHO have to try to analyse and
advise countries on major health sector development
problems. They have to be sure of their facts and
give the best possible advice in the light of the
latest information. They then programme their
technical cooperation and development funds in ways
which best correspond to the policy priorities they
have agreed with their assemblies and governing
bodies. Multilateral negotiations take place over a
programme shared among a number of countries which
is not so contentious, or with represenatives of
multinational corporations, consumer groups and
interested national representatives over the lack
of the availability or undue availability of
certain drugs or infant foods, which may be more
contentious. WHO has to set standards and try to
arrange and verify binding treaties which prevent
the use of certain drugs or chemicals, dangerous to
health. Lastly, it must widen its appeal beyond
governments to non-government organisations and
people in general, especially where innovative new
policies are necessary and governments must bring
their people behind them on the issues, however
willing or unwilling their governments are at the
beginning of the campaign. Such a list of tasks
could be reproduced for each agency. Not all of
these tasks are always so carefully weighted by
each agency and the best methods used.

THREE PROBLEM AREAS WHICH ISOLATE COMMON
INSTITUTIONAL SOLUTIONS

The institutional issues mentioned in the previous
section are best studied and clarified in context.
The context chosen is a separate analysis of three
central problem areas of the contemporary world and
the UN. In these three problem areas all of the
major UN institutions are engaged and many of its
most important agencies. In the Conclusion, the
experience from the three central problem areas can
be pooled to enable some initial judgements to be

passed on preferred institutional solutions.

The first problem area is how to reduce the
huge economic losses which occur from unduly large
swings in the global trade cycle. Can a reformed UN
System better manage the global economy? Would a
better managed global economy allow both developed
and developing countries to make the structural
adjustments necessary in their mutual long term
interest? Currently, the General Assembly and its
Committees, the Economic and Social Council, World
Bank, IMF, UNCTAD, GATT and a number of UN
departments are all involved. How can their efforts
be feasibly rationalised?

The second problem area is rural development.
In that title is contained a history of United
Nations efforts at promoting development. Rural
development becomes all the more a priority, as
development funds shrink and efforts have to be
concentrated where they are most needed. Also rural
development grows in urgency after starvation
relief work has passed its peak and time can be
given to the long term causes of famine. A final
justification for the choice of rural development,
is that it links so closely with growing concerns
to prevent environmental degradation. Can the UN do
more to break through the problems of rural poverty
without further damaging and if possible even
enhancing the quality of the environment? This
problem area introduces all the major development
agencies of the UN System and strikes hard up
against the sensitive point of the agencies single
sector approach and their defficiencies in
coordination.

The third and final problem area is Third
World security and disarmament. Finding an
effective medium for producing greater Third World
security needs little justification. The
credibility of the UN rests on its capability to
reduce international tension and give peace a real
chance. However major steps in nuclear disarmament
can only be made bilaterally between the
superpowers. The UN can provide a forum for
conventional weapons disarmament, especially if
there is some major move towards superpower detente
in nuclear arms. Without more security there can be
no progress on conventional disarmament. Insecurity
and a high arms expenditure reduces the potential
for economic and social development breeding more
insecurity and dragging in the superpowers. More
justification is required as to why, after 40 years
of ineffective effort, there may be some chance now

in making progress. The answer presented is that the political climate is moving in the right direction and the institutional solutions are sufficiently innovative to open up some new approaches. The issues of peace and security in the UN are the proper domain of the Security Council and the General Assembly should be involved only as a result of blockages in the Security Council. However, despite the blockage the permanent members of the Security Council do not want greater involvement of the General Assembly. The question posed is can the Security Council be made more effective despite the continued existence of the negative vote or 'veto'?

<u>Notes to Chapter 2</u>

1. M. Bertrand – "Contribution à une reflexion sur la reforme des Nations Unies", Corps commune d'inspection (JIU/REP/85/9), page 5, para 13.
2. The total UN professional staff has only increased from 2570 in 1976 to 3090 in 1984. All staff including project, extra-budgetary and General Services increased from 22,600 in 1979 to 26,283 in 1984. It looks as if programmes are being spread thinly.
3. Ibid Bertrand, page 33.
4. Davidson Nicol and John Renninger – "The Restructuring of the United Nations Economic and Social System: Background and analysis", Third World Quarterly, January 1982, p.91.
5. R. Jackson – "A Study of the Capacity of the UN Development System", 2 vols. UN New York 1969 (E.70.1.1, 1970) formalised in resolution 2688 XXV of 1970.
6. UN – "Special United Nations Fund For Economic Development (E/2381)", (1953.II B.1).
7. UN – "United Nations Conference on Trade and Employment" Final Act and Related Documents (1948. 11.D.4). Chapter VII.
8. UN "Report of the Ad hoc Committee on the Restructuring of the Economic and Social Sectors of the United Nations", GA/32/34 1978.
9. UN – "A New United Nations Structure for Global Economic Cooperation" (E.75 II. A.7), 1975.
10. UN – "Repertory of Practice of United Nations Organs, Supplement No. 4, (ESO.V.13), 1982, Article 27(2), p.317 and Article 27(3), p.318 and p. 319.

11. See Chapter 5, p.27.
12. My assessment of the total number of comments
     in a single year is taken from the 'Index to
     Comments made by the Committee, by
     Country'(page vii-xvi). The 41 cases for 1985
     comes from the same report, page 35. the
     report is: ILO-"Report of the Committee of
     Experts on the Application of Conventions and
     Reccomendations",ILO Conference 71st. Session,
     1985.
13. ILO-"Report of the Director General", ILO
     Conference 70th. Session,1984,page 25.
14. General Assembly Official Records, A/39/592,
     Table 1.
15. When the EEC Treaty was signed in 1958, the
     existing Common Assembly of the European Coal
     and Steel Community (ECSC) became the European
     Parliamentary Assembly and then European
     Parliament (1962). Up to direct elections in
     1979, members were delegates from their own
     Parliaments. The idea of direct elections was
     included in Article 21 of the ECSC Treaty and
     Article 138 of the EEC 'Treaty of Rome'. See
     Palmer, M. - "The European Parliament",
     Pergamon Press, 1981, Chapter 2.
16. Membership in the Security Council was
     increased from 11 to 15 in 1966 and the ECOSOC
     from 18 to 27 in 1965 and to 54 in 1973.
17. UNDP-"Policy Review: Coordination of Technical
     Cooperation at the Country Level and
     Examination of the Steps Taken by the UNDP to
     Strengthen Coordination in Practice"; Annual
     Report of the Administrator for 1984,
     DP/1985/4, page 21, para 76.
18. Ameri,H.-"Politics and Process in the
     Specialised Agencies of the United Nations",
     Gower, Aldershot, 1982, page 93.
19. Ibid, Bertrand, page 8, para 23.
20. Draft Paper for the International Civil
     Service Commission by the CCABQ
     (ACC/1984/PER/7) of the 2nd February 1984, see
     Table Annex 11. Also relevant is the paper,
     "Promotion Policy", Note by the Federation of
     International Civil Servants Associations
     (FICSA), (ISIC/19/CRP/8) of the 5th.March
     1984, of which see page 3.
21. Cole S.-"Worlds Apart: Technology and
     North/South Relations in the Global
     Economy",UNITAR, Sussex University, 1984.
22. Stoessinger J.G.and Associates - "Financing

the United Nations System",Brookings, 1964,
page 59.

23. Ibid,Stoessinger, page 58.
24. GA/C5/40/16 for the 1985 UN assessment and
World Bank Development Report for 1985 for GNP
for 1983.
25. ICJ Advisory Opinion, "Certain Expenses of the
United Nations"(20 Vll 62); see also chapter
5 and note 16.
26. See Report by the Secretary General -"Current
Financial Crisis of the United
Nations"(A/40/1102) 12 April 1986.
27. GA/40/769, Table G.page 21.

Chapter Three

PROBLEM AREA ONE: GLOBAL ECONOMIC MANAGEMENT

Those who consider the global economic problem
currently serious and potentially a crisis are also
concerned that global institutions are
insufficiently powerful to deal with it. Both the
technical and the political difficulties of global
institutional restructuring will appear
insurmountable until they are outweighed by the
perceived costs of another economic crisis. The
problems of linking multilateral trading and
financial negotiations within the existing
institutional frameworks are indeed formidable. No
one can expect a single agency to concern itself
with the global management of both finance and
trade; even the aborted International Trade
Organisation would not have had that width of
responsibilities. There is nonetheless a perceived
need not only to increase the roles of some of the
existing agencies and either to coordinate or to
combine their secretariats but also to form some
higher level guiding body with an element of
discretionary power, which would establish the
major lines of short and medium-term global
economic management. Only the UN System could or
should fill this gap. Given the balance of economic
and political forces in each relevant agency or
department, no existing part of the System would be
allowed to do so. Should the 1984 economic upturn
prove short-lived, however, the resulting economic
crisis may finally force changes in attitudes. It
is prudent to have feasible alternatives ready.

    Proposals abound for the reform of UN economic
and social institutions, but the failure of the
1975-77 exercise to make significant progress has
produced scepticism about renewed attempts.[1]
Improved efficiency is itself insufficient

44

justification for reform, not only because it
appears to involve increased power (unacceptable to
some of the parties) but also because the
motivation to negotiate in forums provided by the
United Nations has not been present. UN economic
and social institutions must provide useful forums
for negotiation, in itself not easy. More to the
point, governments must be persuaded that they have
enough common interest to negotiate or at the
minimum that certain programmes can be launched,
even without full agreement on specifics.

Conflicting interests have so far proved
irreconcilable at successive international
conferences on North/South problems, especially
where the establishment of a New International
Economic Order was the issue. The recession of
1978-81 and continuing slow growth have weakened
the alliance between oil-rich and other developing
countries. However, new forces now at work are
convincing decision makers that global negotiations
are necessary. The centrepiece will be not a New
International Economic Order but the resolution of
two related problems. First, there are the global
repercussions of the debt-servicing problems of
several major developing countries; second, if the
current upturn in the United States comes
prematurely to an end, the realisation will grow
that long-term global recessionary forces must
worsen. Rumblings at economic summits and in
regional and sectoral forums have been growing
louder since 1982; major support for a "Bretton
Woods" type of conference was given by the
Commonwealth finance ministers in 1983, and
President François Mitterrand also supported the
idea at the Williamsburg summit of 1983.[2]

At the autumn 1984 meeting of the IMF/World
Bank group it was finally decided to hold such a
conference in 1985 without stipulating under whose
auspices it will be held. In fact, no major
conference did result and apart from the 1985 US
Baker Plan to increase the flow of investment to
the debtor countries, the situation rests unchanged.

The global economy is being run below its
productive potential and is subject to unnecessary
swings in finance and trade. A new focus for global
negotiations could be to find a way of keeping the
global economy on a steady growth path, not too far
below its productive potential, and of reducing the
amplitude of the short-term economic trade cycle.
Negotiations over structural changes in trade,
finance, and industrial production can reinforce

45

efforts to raise and to steady global rates of growth, and thus be built into global economic management itself.

THE EXTENT OF THE ECONOMIC PROBLEM

The Financial Crisis

A possible financial crisis is brewing in the developed economies, and one is already present in the developing world. The international institutional response is likely to be inappropriate or ineffective. Even if financial crisis is avoided in the developed countries, the global banking system will sharply contract credit and restrain any tendency toward expansion.[3]
    The global financial crisis stems from two major forces. The first is the urgent debt-service and liquidity problem of some major middle-income developing countries especially those whose oil revenues are dramatically falling with falling oil prices and the growing balance-of-payments problems of a large range of other developing countries. The industrialised market-economy countries are the creditors, and their banks, which have made the loans, are overextended. The risks of bank collapse at the least are worrying and at the worst endager the whole world economy. Most developing countries are restraining their economies, and banks are tightening their cash and reserve holdings. Central banks will without doubt be ready to prevent a panic.
    The global financial system is, however, of uncertain volatility, and central banks are concerned by the cost of protracted rescue operations on domestic reserves, currency values, and standards of probity for commercial banks. Central banks in developed countries have required their national commercial banks to strengthen their cash positions and write down their nonperforming assets. Developing countries have been forced to adjust to high debts by reducing imports and cutting government expenditures.
    The second major force that could lead to global financial crisis is the relative size of the current-account deficit of the United States, which stood at $58 billion for the twelve months ending July 1984.[4] If the United States has to restrain its own current-balance deficit, it substantially reduces the chances for global recovery. Trade over

the last thirty years has greatly altered the shape of the US economy; US imports as a percentage of GDP have increased from 3 percent in 1950 to 10 percent in 1980. The US government will be less opposed to reforms in global financial management once its own current-payments problem starts to impinge on its national economy.

A Derived Crisis

World trade has suffered greatly from the campaign in industrialised countries to reduce inflation. The International Monetary Fund (IMF) is now requiring developing countries to adjust their economies downward, to reduce debt and payments problems, while the industrialised countries are cutting their own imports from developing countries under increasingly strong protectionist regimes. The legacy of the 1979-82 recession is a gradually eroding multilateral trading system where negotiated rounds of tariff reductions have been replaced or neutralised by a varied assortment of nontariff barriers and bilateral agreements that go under the name "managed trading".

World trade declined during the 1979-82 recession, and even the (perhaps optimistic) forecasts of growth by the UN Department of International Economic and Social Affairs (DIESA) for 1984 and 1985, of 4 percent and 5 percent respectively, are lower than might be expected for this stage of an upturn. The cost of monetary constraints in much of the developed world is high in terms of lost trade and output. Monetary contraints were imposed at a time when many developing countries (especially in Latin America), using imported capital from commercial banks, switched from import substitution to production for export.[5] It is not unreasonable to ask how much smaller the difficulties of these countries would have been had monetary constraints not been imposed. Even more important now is the possible effect of a second round of financial constraints. Global economic management may be necessary to break the vicious circle of trade and financial restrictions.[6]

The debt-servicing problems of the developing countries were to some extent an outcome of the global recession and the industrialised countries' method of fighting inflation since 1980. With a less cyclical and a steadier growth in industrialised countries, the developing countries would not have had the inflated growth expectations that led them to incur their current debt burdens. Nor would commercial banks in creditor countries suddenly stop making new loans.

Steadier global economic growth would have provided the foreign-exchange earnings needed to service debts regularly.[7] If the World Bank's target 1985-95 middle-case growth rates of GDP for industrialised countries, 3.8 percent in real terms, had been achieved for the period 1978-84, developing country exports by 1984 would have been $480 billion (assumed inflation of 5 percent and real annual growth of 6.4 percent).[8] The extra net foreign-exchange earnings over actual 1984 earnings of US$80 billion would have covered the debt-service costs of the developing countries.

Harmonisation of global interest-rate policy is required as well as exchange-rate stabilisation. The breakdown of Bretton Woods in 1971 with floating rates has not produced an exchange-rate regime reflecting comparative trade advantage. Despite floating rates, the world has continued to use the dollar as the principal international unit of account. This standard of exchange is threatening to break down, and the resulting financial insecurity is influencing world trade and payments. In the event of a major fall in dollar values, the absence of a stable reserve currency would greatly inhibit trade. One consequence of the highly interdependent trading structure that has grown up over the last twenty years is the decline in the importance of flexible exchange rates as an instrument of national economic policy. No national foreign-exchange regulations are really effective against "currency substitution." A stable global unit of account is essential for an interdependent trading structure to survive. The time is growing more propitious to increase the use of the IMF's Special Drawing Right (SDR) as the major international unit of account (see below) in addition to its use as a reserve asset.

One major difficulty of any attempt at global economic management (GEM) is the amount of trade and finance that lies beyond the control of international trade and payments systems. The unrestrained Eurodollar market provides an example of how credit and liquid assets can grow with economic expansion outside officially controlled banking networks. From the trade side, inter-firm and firm-to-firm subcontracted trade and production have significantly replaced "normal" trade relationships covered, for example, by the rules and regulations of the General Agreement on Tariffs and Trade (GATT). The problem is to make global macroeconomic tools of management effective without imposing an unacceptably tight institutional system of control on either trade or financial markets.

A further problem of global financial management is that it is becoming more difficult to limit the range of questions considered to the short term. For example, structural adjustment to meet IMF conditions has required the Fund to go into many longer-term issues. The developing countries have long been urging the IMF to recognise that their special development problems are not susceptible to financial control methods traditional in industrialised countries. The division of labour between the IMF and the World Bank over short- and long-term loans is becoming more blurred.[9]

THE LIMITS OF GLOBAL ECONOMIC INSTITUTIONS

Whether international economic institutions have sufficient powers is a question that will be answered affirmatively by those who consider the problems under control and who think that a small group of finance ministers and central bankers from developed countries should make the decisions. But the problems surpass the capability of the existing financial system. I propose here that mechanisms should be strengthened and made more broadly representative.

One issue of restructuring is to find a formula that reconciles the current weighted-voting domination of the industrialised countries in the IMF and World Bank, which reflects their economic power, and the developing countries' domination of UN organs such as UNCTAD, by one-country-one-vote procedures. A formula is required sufficiently flexible to allow a rationalisation of the current institutional structure, reduce the number of overlapping functions, and be more adaptable in filling gaps in global economic management as they arise.

Voting formulas are important for international bodies that can take decisions, execute functions and programmes, or give policy guidance. Procedures are more important than voting formulas for bodies such as the GATT, which act mainly as negotiating agencies; votes are hardly

ever taken in the GATT, resolutions seldom put
forward. The governing councils of bodies that will
need to carry out GEM will have to be concerned
with both voting and working procedures.

The Concept of Global Economic Management

It would be a major step forward for the
international community to agree there should be
GEM, to decide on its limits and the tools to be
used and the division of discretionary powers
between the relevant secretariats and the
decision-making bodies. Some recent literature has
supported the general concept, but it has not
explored the details of different objectives and
negotiating positions of the parties to the
decisions.[10] Most of the discussion has been
less about GEM than about such longer-term
development issues as increasing the quantity of
SDRs and IMF/World Bank Loan capital or a new Third
World Bank's soft loan capability.
  The objective of GEM is to stabilise the
global economy on a chosen growth path. This
objective is very different from the outcome of
Bretton Woods, which was for equilibrium in
exchange rates and the short-run balance of
payments (IMF) and long-run growth (World
Bank).[11] The Keynes plan for an international
currency would have included GEM, but it was not
accepted.[12]
  The growth path chosen would have to conform
to some acceptable agreement on global and hence
regional absorptive capacity (a rate that did not
produce excessive resource constraints and
inflationary trends). GEM would involve a number of
related activities:

  a forecasting mechanism to produce global
  growth rates;
  a negotiating process over a global (and
  regional) growth rate on which international
  organisations would base their economic
  management;
  activities of global monetary and development
  institutions to control the supply of funds to
  countries;
  and negotiations over structural adjustments
  to achieve the agreed growth rates, both at
  various multinational levels, for issues of
  broad interest where multicountry bargaining

is required, and at the level of the
individual country.

The clear front-runner in any choice of options is
some enlarged use of the IMF's SDR as a unit of
account, a fund of last resort, and a reserve
currency. The SDR is the only feasible weapon where
general rules could be made which would allow the
secretariat a reasonable range of discretion about
the extent of its use at any one time. Other
monetary, fiscal, and trade interventions would all
need to be negotiated with individual countries. As
long as the SDR was made a sufficiently powerful
lever, however, these other country-based tools of
policy could be negotiated. Global monetary weapons
by themselves, even acting through interest rates,
are crude techniques for controlling the global
economy, but if they existed, governments might be
persuaded to use more effective and less crude
techniques to arrive at the same ends more
equitably and more efficiently.
    The classic weapon of national central banks
is their open-market operations, selling securities
to reduce liquidity, lower bond prices, and raise
interest rates and the reverse if a more
expansionary credit policy is desired. SDRs could
be used for this purpose to buy securities if they
were acceptable and tradable commercially or if
they had to be accepted as part of a contractual
agreement between the IMF and central banks.[13]
The four billion SDRs held internally by the IMF
are insufficient for the IMF to acquire a stock of
securities; there would have to be a large new
issue of SDRs which could then be used by the Fund
to acquire securities in response to agreed GEM
expansionary objectives.[14]
    SDRs can be issued only under stringent
controls by the executive council of the IMF and
not as part of countercyclical policy. No
arrangement exists for their repurchase. Central
banks used SDRs less once the dollar recovered from
its devaluation in 1971; SDRs would probably have
to become more commercially acceptable,
irrespective of the market's faith in the dollar,
before central banks would willingly hold large
quantities. There are also technical problems in
making SDRs freely tradable and therefore more
acceptable as a major reserve currency, but they
are solvable.[15]
    The political problems of using SDRs as a
reserve currency will fade if the market does lose

faith in the dollar. European objections to using
SDRs as a reserve currency would diminish if the
quantity in circulation is more closely related to
a process of GEM that itself has received prior
approval. Then the "link" between the issue of SDRs
and development will depend on other explicit
factors and the inflationary risks be contained.
The global level of open-market operation and its
country disaggregation is both technically and
politically a delicate problem. It should be
unnecessary to reach a technical consensus on the
required level of open-market operations for
specific countries prior to national-level
negotiations. As far as possible consensus should
be reached for global and regional open-market
operations, leaving country negotiations in the
hands of the secretariat of the responsible
international agencies, which would take into
account all other adjustment measures.

The technical weapons of GEM, therefore, are
not only open-market operations but any of the
weapons available nationally to reflate or deflate
the economy. Also, open-market operations would not
be the only international lever to obtain economic
adjustment; they would be added to the short- and
long-term loans and other copartnership loans of
the IMF/World Bank group. Altogether these various
tools of management would make up a rather powerful
and potent mixture.

Reviews and Forecasting

A great deal of global economic forecasting and
analytical work is currently undertaken within the
United Nations and specialised agencies and by
private bodies; global modelling under DIESA, the
World Bank, and the ILO, regular trade and
development reviews by UNCTAD, the World
Development Report by the World Bank, the World
Economic Outlook by the IMF, the UN World Economic
Survey Reports, and many others. Some of these,
however, are produced with special interests in
mind and are insufficiently geared to the specific
policy options open for GEM. (As there has been no
capability for GEM, so the absence of material to
guide it is hardly surprising.) Nevertheless,
these are powerful tools for carrying out GEM, and
the main problem would be coordinating and
rationalising the work.

Without going into issues of who does what in
the secretariat (addressed on page 60), there

52

is a need for a careful review of global economic short-term trends, a trend forecast, and some growth options based on different levels or structures of GEM. Supporting this exercise should be independent but closely coordinated economic research, which would improve the whole technical side of the GEM process (the World Institute for Development Research under the UN University has been formed with this specific objective in mind). A politically acceptable negotiating forum is also required, one that could consider the options presented and make a choice sufficiently clear to guide the following process steps and subsequent executive action by agencies and secretariats.

Forums for Decisions on GEM

Neither the IMF/World Bank group (Development Committee) nor a UN institution such as UNCTAD would provide a forum acceptable to both industrialised and developing countries. The issues are too wide to be left to the Interim Committee of the IMF, the high-level committee that mainly represents the interests of central banks and finance ministries. The Interim Committee was set up to consider and decide on reforms originally prepared by the IMF "Committee of Twenty". Both the Committee of Twenty and the Executive Board of the IMF were considered by industrialised countries to be too unwieldy and low level, despite weighted voting.[16] The United States and other industrialised countries, which strongly favour this body, will be willing to compromise with the developing countries only with the possibility of a changed economic and political climate.

Apart from these actual and potential financial and economic forces, there are the political changes that may also arise from a thaw in East-West relations. The issue of improving bank clearance and exchange arrangements between East and West banking systems will come to the surface if and when relations improve. The GEM forums and institutions must not neglect to incorporate East-West balance as well as North-South.

Any acceptable and successful forum that considered restructuring would probably become the principal decision-making body in the restructured system. Once such a conference on restructuring is under way, there will be considerable pressure to compromise on an institution that can make decisions acceptable to developed and developing countries alike. No single existing UN or other intergovernmental agency quite matches requirements.

The major concern is to preserve enough heterogeneity in the institutional system so that a monolithic decision-making structure is not created, but not to weaken the structure so greatly that binding decisions and agreements cannot be reached. As Miriam Camps has written, the process toward heterogeneity has gone too far; it is possible to have a few strong, well-organised global institutions that have chambers, tiers and inner groups to allow for negotiations between the closely interested parties.[17] As Robert Rothstein argues, it is possible to overcome the rigidity of negotiations between small representative groups by preceding negotiations with secretariat or expert-group advice and option presentation, and following small-group sessions with a plenary session circumscribed by rules that limit its right to amend or take apart the agreements reached.[18] It is also possible to have a higher-level forum confining itself to negotiations that give a policy direction to other existing executive institutions. One initial solution for the high-level forum would be to find some blend between two existing bodies, accepting double representation as part of the compromise; for example, the IMF/World Bank Development Committee could be temporarily combined with either UNCTAD/Trade and Development Board or the Second Committee of the General Assembly, with the former undertaking the initial negotiations and the latter the later discusssions, but with the proviso that both must approve the final documents.[19] Such a compromise would be easier to achieve than proposals for a completely new body. Over time the working relation between the two bodies would be streamlined, and the resulting amalgamation could constitute a single forum (albeit, perhaps, with two chambers). What therefore is being sought is less the identification of an individual forum than a whole process.

THE GEM PROCESS

The new forum would have functions on the international economic scene at a higher level than existing agencies and organisations. These existing organisations (World Bank, IMF, GATT, UNCTAD,

UNIDO) would have tacitly or explicitly to accept the forum's guidance. The implications for the UN Economic and Social Council and the Second Committee of the General Assembly are more profound and are discussed on page 62.

There would be differing impacts on existing secretariats and some rationalisation of functions; a few of the agency "barons" might well resist some aspects of rationalisation, and it will require high-level delegate agreement in the initial meetings to overcome the influence of their patronage and lobbying.

The GEM Formulation Conference

The double forum suggested above would meet to discuss and make the principal initial decisions; the two bodies could meet separately and in a plenary forum, with sufficient opportunity for informal meetings. The papers to be considered at the formulation conference would concentrate on the process of global economic management. Other North-South subjects would cloud the issues at the initial stage; they might be considered in later mettings of the conference, then be reconstituted and regularised as part of the GEM process.

This formulation conference would differ from later meetings of the forum to agree on global and regional growth rates and to bargain over multicountry trade and financial and industrial adjustment issues. The initial conference agrees the broad principles and programmes of a GEM process and constitutes the institutions that will operate it. Agreement on process before discussing the burning issues that have brought the parties together may not satisfy everyone, but no single conference is likely both to agree the GEM process and to settle the issues involved in structural adjustment. The argument that the GEM process itself would ease the path of global adjustment negotiations is the key to this order of activities.

Immediate institutional changes need go just so far as is necessary to achieve the objectives of an orderly GEM process, bringing together the forecasting services of existing agencies of the UN System, the decision and negotiating councils of the IMF/World Bank group, the GATT, and UNCTAD, the executive cordination of IMF Special Drawing Rights and World Bank loan policies and national-level programming, and the establishment of a GEM process secretariat. The immediate institutional changes are, therefore, not large except for the specific open-market operations of the IMF (on which IMF staff work is well advanced). In the agencies the arranging of joint meetings of such bodies as the IMF/World Bank group Development Committee with the UNCTAD/Trade and Development Board is a major step. Secretariat cooperation to forecast global and regional growth and suggest levels of intervention, and Bank group/UN cooperation at country-level negotiations over structural adjustments, are from the point of view of the agencies also very considerable institutional changes. Governments, however, will not see them as so different from current agency structures. The pressure for agreement on a GEM process and the continuing high-level forum meetings will ensure the growing strength and permanence of interagency arrangements; in the long term the institutional changes are likely to be more profound.

The papers for the formulation conference would be kept to a minimum and perhaps could be limited to three. One would relate the current debt crisis, financial uncertainty, increasing protectionism, and slow growth to ineffective global economic management. The second would outline a possible management process, linking agreement on acceptable global and regional growth rates to general and national-level structural adjustment negotiations and to the control weapons of the IMF/World Bank group. The third would discuss purely institutional arrangements and propose an initial budget for a forum secretariat and forum meetings. It would clarify the legal basis of decisions reached in the forum, the executive limits of the secretariat, and in particular the strengthened IMF's role, acting as a global central bank.

GEM Decision Making

The GEM process could consist of four levels of activity. First would be analysis and technical-level discussion of global trends and growth options. Second would be a regular annual forum and negotiations over the choice of growth options. Third would be the parallel forum negotiations over "group" economic adjustments. Fourth would be bilateral and detailed country-level negotiations and adjustment agreements. The decisions resulting from these processes require clarification.

Technical-level Discussions Over Growth Options.
The forum will be presented with a technical-level
review by the secretariat, with an expert
commentary. The form of the review will be to
present a small number of options based on
achievements made in financial and structural
adjustments. The secretariat would not make
decisions, simply recommendations to the forum.

Regular Forum Discussions Over Choice of Growth
Options. At the end of its annual discussions the
forum will have to choose global and regional
growth options as the working basis for the
secretariat and later structural adjustment
meetings. Thus the forum would decide either
optimistically, believing it can achieve a great
deal in its structural adjustment meetings, or
pessimistically, if (perhaps at the early stages)
it believed that only a little progress can be
made. Whatever voting procedure was agreed to
decide the growth targets, a positive vote would be
sufficient for the secretariat and the Bank group.
Once power was given to the IMF as a central bank
to conduct open-market operations, only outright
refusal to accept the purchases and sales of SDRs
as a basis of credit policy by particular central
banks could give meaning to dissenting votes. If a
powerful country were to use its financial strength
to oppose the work of the IMF in this case it is
difficult to foresee the outcome. It is doubtful
that one country acting alone could break the
System; it is likely that it would have to "opt
out" and take the consequences of increasing
isolation.

General Negotiations to Make Economic Adjustments.
Feasible broad packages of adjustment proposals can
be prepared and put before the forum with
recommended "trade-offs" for groups of countries;
these packages would be strongly related to
short-term, GEM-required adjustments but would
explicitly refer to longer-term development
objectives approved in other international forums.
The trade-offs would deliberately aim at cutting
across the lines of existing agencies
(IMF/GATT/UNCTAD) and at providing a lead to these
agencies in their own separate discussions.
    Subjects for initial discussion are those
which link the possibility of increased loans and
of reduced financial restrictions with increased

trade and reduced protectionism. Broad bargaining
packages can be prepared linking key countries and
commodities, with the aim of freeing trade while
maintaining growth or employment levels.
Considerable skill, patience, and flexibility would
be required in putting together the packages and
negotiating them.[20]
    Whether such issues as the international
transfer of technology, industry, and skilled
labour should enter the discussion would depend
upon their clear relation to particular
negotiations on protection and trade restrictions.
It would also depend on the extent to which these
issues were already explored by other agencies such
as UNCTAD or the GATT, so that they were ready to
be included in a bargaining package.
    Decisions reached in these general,
multicountry negotiations would take the form of
international conventions with signatures required
from the negotiating parties to the convention.
Negotiation would be time-bound, to influence next
years's global growth assumptions and to reduce the
pressures on current individual country-level
negotiations for all the parties signing the
convention. There would be more pressure from the
countries to reach a conclusion on a particular
negotiation, compared with current trade
negotiations, than from the secretariat. In current
negotiations, the secretariat frequently has to
find ways to bring the process to a conclusion.

Country-level Negotiations and Adjustments. The GEM
process to stabilise the global economy on a growth
path and the high-level multilateral adjustment
negotiations covering a number of broad areas will
ease the painfulness of economic adjustments
required nationally. I argue strongly for the
retention of "conditionality" in country-level
negotiations, but with two differences. Not only
are national development aims to be taken into
account, which is already increasingly the case (as
a result of continuous lobbying by Third World
countries and the work of the Committee of
Twenty),[21] but so are annual GEM forum decisions.
Developing countries have criticised not
conditionality as such, but the manner in which it
is used; these proposals recognise their
justifiable concerns.
    From time to time, and with considerable
discretion, the IMF or the World Bank holds
negotiations with an industrialised country over

its short- or long-term economic situation. With
the advent of GEM many more such negotiations might
be expected, entailing considerable acceptance by
industrialised countries not only of the GEM
process but of the discretion and integrity of
secretariat teams that carried it out. Secretariat
work in this area would increase.

Secretariat Rationalisation for the GEM Process

Global Trends and Growth Options: Forecasting Could
be Rationalised. Too many UN agencies currently
produce economic reviews. One reasonably
comprehensive annual review, benefiting from the
resources and experience of each, could do for all
of them.[22] In this case of rationalisation the
claims of heterogeineity are unjustified; main
disagreements can be translated into options and
covered by the mode of presentation. Anyway, the
benefits of a clear focus for policy are so great
as to outweigh any benefits from having each agency
producing its own report. The first step in
coordination is to ensure the GEM process review is
carried out with inputs from both DIESA, ILO (World
Employment Programme), UNCTAD, and the IMF/World
Bank group. It will take high-level decisions to
obtain secretariat agreement on even this
apparently reasonable step in agency coordination.
DIESA might appropriately coordinate the production
of the review, using as a secretariat base the team
that already writes the annual World Economic
Survey. Secondments to the production team and a
review committee could be made from the other
contributing agencies, using statistical data
collected by each. An external commentary on the
review presented by DIESA could be submitted to the
decision forum (along with the DIESA review) by the
UN Committee of Planners to add greater weight to
the forecasts, as a lot more will depend upon them
than on other forecasts made by the agencies. The
economists and economic statisticians of the UN
System could greatly increase their contribution to
the formation of global economic policy.

Secretariat Services to the Forum. The choice of
arrangements for forum secretariat services is to
some extent governed by the nature of the
negotiations that will take place in the forum. The
main difficulty is that the IMF/Bank group staff
representatives are a party to the negotiations and
not just members of the secretariat.

A secretariat team is required which represents and assists the country-group representatives in their negotiations both with the IMF/Bank group and among themselves. Some members of the IMF/Bank group could be in the temporary forum secretariat team, among them those who assisted with the annual review and growth option papers as well as country advisers on money and fiscal or structural economic areas (industry, trade and agriculture, etc.). These individuals should appreciate their temporary allegiance to the forum secretariat team leader. The most senior IMF/Bank group staff would, on the other hand, represent their organisations (or, more optimistically, the Bank group as a whole).

With such an arrangement the forum secretariat would best be placed under the direct guidance of a small high-level group led by the UN Director-General for Development. The operative management team leader could come from any of the agencies but with team members drawing on the seconded skills of the Bank group, UNCTAD, GATT, ILO, DIESA, and UNIDO as required. Members would be seconded for the meeting as well as allowed sufficient time for preparation and writing up. The forum budget would need to include salary costs for seconded agency members.

The budget of the forum secretariat would initially have to be covered by voluntary contributions from countries and existing agencies. However, one useful innovation would be some cost recovery of secretariat expenses through a charge on the increase in SDR and loan activities of the Bank group and a fee contribution from the functional organisations represented at trade and labour negotiations.

<u>Country-level Negotiations and Adjustments</u>.
Secretariat functions for negotiating adjustments at the country level need to be streamlined; it is unnecessary for countries to undergo successive investigations by both the IMF and the World Bank. The programming staff of the World Bank and the IMF do in fact frequently have a similar timeframe and cover overlapping areas.[23] Since open-market operations and structural adjustment loans need to be negotiated with each country, in relation to its structure and development programme and problems in context, joint programming will greatly benefit the succeeding negotiations.

As at present, regularly scheduled joint Bank/IMF negotiations at the country level, annually or biannually, would be held at the request of the group not the forum. Because countries can offer alternative policy solutions in exchange for open-market operations and loans, countries should have the opportunity to conduct bilateral bargaining with the IMF/World Bank group with the aid of a member of the forum secretariat. Experts on trade or sectoral adjustment questions may be welcomed by both countries and the IMF/Bank group to assist with the negotiations. The objective of a secretariat presence at a country negotiation with the IMF/World Bank group would be to facilitate the negotiation, not to represent either side. Governments could always make separate requests (and to the same organisations) for officers on technical cooperation to support them. There would be a case for strengthening the funds available for this purpose from UNDP/UNDTC.

THE IMPLICATIONS FOR THE UNITED NATIONS

A forum interleaving the governing bodies of the IMF/World Bank group and a representative body of UN member countries is a UN System restructuring solution, predicated on the assumption that it is still too early for any fundamental reforms of UN economic and social institutions. The forum would, however, not only pave the way for real global negotiations and the possible establishment of a GEM process, it would also provide an alternative path to later, more fundamental UN structural reforms. The implications for the future of the IMF/World Bank group, ECOSOC, UNCTAD, and the GATT are profound. A framework will be provided for rationalising the secretariats of these bodies, which if it were not carefully planned would nevertheless happen by attrition; agencies not wanting to cooperate would find their secretariats bypassed.
　　　　The introduction of the governing bodies of the IMF/World Bank group into the forum has a triple intention. First, it strengthens the industrialised countries' willingness to negotiate. Second, it provides a medium in the longer term to democratise the group's secretariat, which is one of the important parties to the negotiations. Third, it strengthens the bridge between the Eastern bloc and the IMF/World Bank group, which is currently weak. In the short run it would benefit both the Bank group's secretariat and the UN secretariats to share roles in the forum

negotiations. In the longer run there is the
question as to whether the Bank group secretariat
should be separate from the forum because it is
party to the negotiations.

The industrialised countries' greater
confidence in the Bank group's secretariat is
likely to overrule any worry about the growth of
supranational power in the forum secretariat.
Perhaps the more difficult problem will be if the
industrialised countries do not want the United
Nations to share in the long-term secretariat of
the forum. The original rationale for the
compromise creating the forum should be the
convincing argument.

The relation between decisions reached by the
forum and the UN General Assembly is a complicating
factor. The Economic and Social Council of the
United Nations submits its decisions to the General
Assembly. Because the Security Council has a
relationship to the General Assembly on political
issues parallel to what the proposed forum would
have on economic issues, we might assume that the
forum would report to, but not submit its decisions
to, the General Assembly. The whole issue could
initially be avoided by tacit consent until it was
seen how well the forum operated and decisions were
made on the long-term future of ECOSOC.

ECOSOC in the longer term would be able to
allocate most of its functions to either the forum
or one of the committees of the General Assembly.
Most economic negotiations involving decisions of
member countries, rather than decisions affecting
only UN agencies, could eventually be taken in the
forum. If the General Assembly committees were to
replace some of the ECOSOC functions there would be
a case for amalgamating the Second and Third
Committees, explicitly making a development role
covering both economic and social sectors.

The negotiating functions of UNCTAD four-year
conferences would also pass to the forum. Much of
the detailed work and negotiations on specific
commodities, services, or manufactures would take
place in greater association with the GATT. If the
forum succeeded in encouraging real negotiations as
well as GEM, some of the pressure for exclusive
negotiations to take place in either UNCTAD or the
GATT would be removed. The industrialised countries
and developing countries may want their own meeting
places; they may even require their own
secretariats; but the focus of negotiation need not
be UNCTAD or the GATT separately. The case for a

combined trade organisation would become overwhelming.

Secretariats seconded to the forum would eventually end up as full-time members of the forum secretariat. Among them would be the forecasting experts on industry in UNIDO and on world employment in the ILO. Because of the need for much more participation of the forum in bilateral negotiations at the country level, however, representatives of the ILO or UNIDO may well be seconded to maintain agency involvement and reduce forum secretariat costs.

IMPACT OF GEM ON GROWTH AND DEVELOPMENT

Any institutional restructing of the UN system depends upon a change in the economic and political climate. The leading governments of power blocks will have to perceive a converging interest toward an institutional or programme innovation, however well pressented, before they will accept it. Economic trends could bring such a change about within the next year or two. The predicted rise in the US foreign deficit, followed by a falling dollar and renewed recession, will more favourably predispose developed countries toward international community initiatives.

Especially important are the responses of the US government, which still hopes to expand out of both internal and external deficits. European governments have not in the recent past followed US economic policy changes, but because their economies have never really pulled out of the last recession they are already more willing to listen to international policy advice. Further conservative reaction to the crisis will only deepen the recession and sharpen the volte-face when it comes.And when it does, a UN framework for a solution may be the least painful of the alternatives, not only because there are few national or regional policy alternatives left untried but also because the international option lies somewhat to the side of major changes in national policy.

Global economic management might have considerably reduced the impact of the recessions of 1974-75 and 1981-82, although the petrodollar recycling problem would still have proved structurally intractable. GEM might also have modified levels of inflation between 1975 and 1980, depending on how much structural adjustment

63

countries accepted. The impact of GEM could have altered the whole political climate itself, turning it from greater confrontation between North and South and between East and West toward détente and mutually beneficial economic trade-offs. The social costs of GEM foregone are thus very high.

The solution recommended is not to be typified as international Keynesianism. First, pure Keynesian solutions would be insufficiently innovative at the inflationary end of the cycle in controlling "near-money" (i.e., the Eurocurrency market). Second, they would not have attempted to provide leverage for dialogue at the national level to break through social and structural rigidities (i.e., cost-push inflation). Third, they are less concerned with stimulating long-term structural and secular development. The solution proposed aims to cover all these points by the interaction increasingly required between national and international monetary and development institutions. In dealing with cyclical depression Keynesian solutions are a clear priority; the need now to think more widely than Keynesian solutions when pulling out of recession does not excuse remaining in recession to avoid being labelled Keynesian.

Notes to Chapter 3

1. For a critical review see Davidson Nicol and John Renniger, "The Restructuring of the United Nations Economic and Social System: Background and Analysis," Third World Quarterly, January 1982.
2. See Towards a New Bretton Woods: Challenges for the World Financial and Trading System (London: Commonwealth Secretariat, 1983).
3. This thesis is clearly stated in Robert McNamara's reprinted Barbara Ward Memorial Lecture, in Anne Mattis, ed., SID Prospectus 1982 (Durham: Duke University Press, 1983).
4. Economist, 21-27 July 1984, p. 94.
5. Some South Asian countries with an existing export base or lower debt-service ratios were less vulnerable to the trade recession.
6. Global economic management is distinct from "managed trade regimes" which are bilateral and mainly restrictive.
7. From World Bank data in World Development Report 1983, Figure 3.2.

8. Even with World Bank low-growth case of 2.5% per annum, industrialised countries' GDP would have yielded the developing countries an extra $40 billion. The high-case industrialised countries' growth rate of GDP of 5.0% per annum would have increased 1984 exports in developing countries over actual 1984 by $170 billion, perhaps nearly as unacceptably inflationary as the current actual (and to a lesser extent, the World Bank low-case) rates were recessionary.

9. Surveillance under Article IV of the Fund Agreement is no longer to prevent monetary restrictions and multiple currency arrangements but to examine the policies that lie behind exchange rates; IMF Annual Report, 1983, pp. 61-65.

10. See, for example, Stein Rossen, "Notes on Rules and Mechanisms Governing International Economic Relations" (Chr. Michelsen Inst., DERAP, 1981); F. Stewart and A. Sengupta, Internaional Financial Cooperation: A Framework for Change (Boulder: Westview, 1982); and M. Camps, Collective Management: The Reform of Global Economic Organisations (New York: McGraw-Hill, 1980).

11. Any once-and-for-all increase in the issue of new SDRs or their "link" to developing country finance problems has to be considered in terms of the new GEM objective.

12. Miriam Camps in Collective Management clarified the ambiguity in the concept of a global central bank that would preserve a fixed exchange rate, create international reserves, "affect" or "control" money supplies, and to a greater or lesser extent, conduct countercyclical policy. Not every economist who writes about a global central bank means the same thing.

13. If central banks agreed a fixed ratio between their SDR holdings and other reserves, a small SDR issue could control a large global reserve structure; this is known as the Witteveen Proposal, after the IMF's managing director who put it forward in 1978.

14. IMF Annual Report, 1983, Appendix VIII. SDRs held by participants were 17 billion, still only 5% of total world reserve assets (including gold).

15. W.R. Coats, "The SDR as a Means of Payment:

Reply to Comments," IMF Staff Papers, September 1983.

16. For the report of the Committee of Twenty, see IMF, International Monetary Reform (Washington, D.C.,1974).

17. Ibid, Camps, Collective Management.

18. R.L. Rothstein, "Is the North-South Dialogue Worth Saving?" Third World Quarterly, January 1984.

19. Even considering the very great political problems involved, special efforts would be required to ensure further strengthening of the Eastern Bloc (CMEA) countries in the IMF/World Bank Development Committee. Double representation in the forum would achieve the compromise between North and South but not wholly satisfy the required balance between East and West. The Development Committee has more opportunities for flexible membership than the Bank group governing bodies.

20. Preconditions for successful negotiations have been studied by J. Sewell and I.W. Zartman in "Global Negotiations: Path to the Future or Dead End Street," Third World Quarterly 6 (April 1984).

21. Finally resulting in the second change to the IMF Articles of Agreement in April 1978.

22. A review of these models is long overdue but requires separate attention and research.

23. The World Bank has both programming and project staff. The first group works with countries on short- and medium-term economic forecasts and analysis of relevant economic and development problems. The programming carried out by countries with the UNDP is to allocate the UNDP's mainly technical cooperation funds.

Chapter Four

PROBLEM AREA TWO: RURAL DEVELOPMENT AND THE
ENVIRONMENT

Improvements in performance of the UN System in
economic and social development can usefully be
studied by focussing on rural development as a
major problem area. The institutional weaknesses of
the UN System in the one development area are
possible clues to, and illustrations of, more
widespread weaknesses. The problem chosen is a key
one because, if widely interpreted to cover all
development aims, both national and international,
in developing country rural areas, then it embraces
a large part of the UN and specialised agency
development functions. There is therefore a double
objective in writing this chapter; to strike a blow
for the UN System and for rural development.
     In discussing the effectiveness of the UN
System it is important to look at the distinctive
features of the governance and structure of the UN
and its specialised agencies. In particular the
relatively wide limits of action of each of the
governing bodies of the agencies is regarded as an
underrated potential in comparison with their
assemblies and the full-time secretariats. The
question is posed, if there has not been clarity of
focus and internal coordination of effort for rural
development within the UN System, who carries most
responsibility, the political side of the
assemblies and their governing bodies, the
secretariat, or does all the fault lie at the
country level?
     A perceptive UNDP evaluation study[1] lamented
that all too often:

     "rural development tends to be viewed as a
     definable set of programmes that government,
     with external cooperation in some cases,
     initiate and control themselves. The concept

of rural development as a process of far reaching political, economic and social transformation of agrarian society, and of agrarian society as the core of the Third World national development, rarely emerges".

The UN System itself has been unable to move effectively from support for particular programmes to an effective medium for assisting countries in the wider tasks of "economic and social transformation of agrarian society." Even with a fully effective UN System and clear focus of effort from headquarters to regional offices, and to country level, the opposition to the wider conceptual meaning of 'rural development' should not be underestimated; it involves changing existing rural power bases, frequently land reform, and protection of rural ecosystems against too rapid encroachment from the large business sector.

Remedial works by UN System agencies for famine, refugees, and to help neglected minorities, will always be required in a world of complex and shifting power groups, where the struggle to reduce inequalities between and within nations is likely to ebb and flow, but never stop. However, the question should be asked, if the UN System today was as effective as it could be, given the existing political pressures and balances of power, would there be less need for narrow programme concepts of rural development and remedial programmes for particular target groups? The answer could be given that it is the current political pressures which keep the UN from realising its potential, but is this not just an excuse? The problems of rural neglect and urban imbalance are growing to such proportions that any chance of making a more effective impact by means of the UN System should be explored.

The developing country model assumes conflicts of interest within countries where very frequently the heads of states and some important ministers as well as many officers of the Civil Service, public sector and non-government agencies would welcome additional support for poverty reduction programmes. It is argued here that the UN has not been able to provide the kind of support for those who are working for rural development and that a change in methods and approach is therefore necessary.

68

THE SCALE OF RURAL DEVELOPMENT PROBLEMS

In the preface to his Annual Report for 1983 IFAD
President, Dr A-Sudeary pointed out that "in spite
of the urgency of the problems of poverty and
hunger, the flow of resources to agriculture and
rural development in developing countries appears
to be falling." In the least developed countries
especially, where nearly all the government's
development budget is from external sources, there
is no excuse for either the international community
or the national administrations to blame the other;
each must look to its role. Within external
official development assistance to developing
countries, the multinational agencies contribute
25%[2] and their potential ability to lead and
organise co-financing multiplies their influence.
Cannot a greater impact be made by more
sharply focussing development efforts? Could not
rural development make more of a contribution to
reducing rural poverty, population growth rates,
gaps in urban rural conditions of life, and
providing more and varied rural employment? Would
not these extra efforts favorably and significantly
impact, in turn, the unbalanced growth of the large
cities, some part of the refugee migrations,
problems of soil erosion, desertification, landless
or marginal farmers and national food security? A
comprehensive review of interdependent factors
involved in ecology and environment changes in the
Third World is given each year by the World Watch
Institute [3] and the United Nations Environement
Programme(UNEP)[4].
What is so striking is that the negative
forces are now predominant compared with the
relatively small efforts that are being made both
by national and international agencies. Yet there
are sufficient signs from successful low cost
replicable programmes in small scale farming,
primary health care, literacy, women's development,
non-formal education, non-agricultural employment,
public works and others, that many of the paths and
pitfalls are known.
This is not the place to outline detailed
national and international strategies for rural
development, but enough will be indicated to
evaluate the current and potential UN contribution.
Sceptics about the range of coverage of rural
development, even used in the widest sense of broad
coverage and capability for replication, need to be

satisfied. Programmes of rural development have
tended to concentrate on raising the productivity
of middle income small farmers (through 'green
revolutionary' technologies), so that the standard
of living of poorer groups is either not improved
at all or may be even worsened. Sceptics will ask
who benefits from rural development.[5] Rural
development programmes can ignore the rural poor
and leave them to other programmes, or the strategy
can embrace them. In the former case, programmes
targeted at special poverty groups are a kind of
social welfare net. In the latter case, rural
development strategies can be oriented so that no
major groups are omitted.

To produce the kind of community based rural
development which embraces all groups requires a
very special national and international support
infrastructure. Many individual national sector
programmes, under their respective sector
ministries, supported by the international
agencies, have attempted to establish their own
support structure, when in fact many of the
problems and needs are the same(management,
communications, leadership motivation, training,
transport, logistics of supply distribution, social
needs surveys, appropriate technology level
appreciation). The costs of providing such common
infrastructures is prohibitive and in many cases is
neglected as much for this as for other, perhaps
more political, reasons. Taking just one known
example of Primary Health Care, supplies, transport
and supervising or referral communication is a
heavy cost burden, if no other government sector
shares in the costs. But to establish the shared
transport, supplies and communications networks
requires decentralised administration, management
development, leadership motivation, training and a
logistical plan; it is not just a case of sharing
final costs. Further, at the delivery end is the
community, with each sector or agency and sometimes
even a division of an agency (where there are
uncoordinated vertically organised programmes),
trying to unload their activities on to a handful
of community leaders and activists. Sometimes at
the national level, especially where there is a
Ministry of Rural or Community Development, the
question of multipurpose community workers is given
consideration, but it is unpopular with sector
ministries and most international sector agencies.

Even more important than a common technical
infrastructure to support the kind of rural

development which embraces all social groups is the strong political and mangerial networks which underpin the infrastructures. This network of rural development leaders can be found at many levels in most pluralistic societies and only the most ruthless systems will have eliminated them. However, many are dormant because they remain insufficiently supported. The Society for International Development 1984 special report on rural development[6] draws attention to this aspect of UN support for rural development within rural communities and in the national or sub-national administrations. In the same reference, Mary Hollensteiner advocates UN organisations siding with the committed individuals and groups and protecting them from outside attacks. Only in this way can vertical, remedial, target directed programmes be avoided and cross sectoral, replicable rural development programmes be adequately supported. It is at the national level of UN System representation that the network has to be plotted and kept constantly up to date and it is at the national level where the UN System of support eventually comes together on behalf of the network.

STRUCTURE AND POLICY FOCUS OF UN SYSTEM AGENCIES

The ability and willingness of UN agencies to focus on rural development is influenced by their structure, their funding sources, size of budget and whether they control their own technical cooperation funds. The table below shows some of these differences for selected agencies.

The World Bank is dependent on the developed countries for votes and the market for funds. IDA, UNDP, IFAD and UNICEF, require developed country voluntary funding subscriptions from governments and for votes, IDA is also dependent on the developed countries. IFAD voting structure is carefully balanced. Whereas UNDP and UNICEF voting is weighted to the developing countries, the indeterminate nature of voluntary subscription funding places de-facto control of agencies dependent on it very much in the hands of the developed countries.

For the specialised agencies, WHO, ILO, FAO, the fixed percentage government financial contributions with developing countries having the majority votes allows ultimate control to rest more firmly in the hands of the developing countries.

The developed countries can take up a major issue and threaten to leave the organisations, but this is rather a heavy weapon to use for discrete policy control. However, more equal voting balances exist in the governing bodies of these organisations as is suggested in the next section.

ILO has the highest proportion of technical cooperation activities financed by UNDP, 47%. Only about 30% of the technical cooperation programmes of FAO is funded by UNDP; the other agencies are even less dependent on UNDP so that, even if UNDP wanted to exert leverage over the agencies to give more focus to technical cooperation programmes, its ability to do so is relatively small.

The result of the constitutional and structural differences in the specialised agencies has been to create varying styles and approaches; however, there are some recent signs of a convergence in approach. This could be due both to technical and political reasons, technical because there is a common appreciation of the inter-sectoral nature of most rural area programmes, the need to work at a level in countries where replication is possible, and political in that open criticism of agencies' delivery capacity has spread sufficiently to justify changes in direction.

UNICEF in the past has been highly successful in focussing its projects on target groups, but has needed to maintain a high visibility to keep up donor interest. It has frequently by-passed national delivery capacity and implemented projects with its own staff. However, it has had the leverage and independence as a result to work through non-government channels. World Bank has used its leverage for limited area poverty focussed projects but also found itself subverting local administration by superimposing its own staff. Only WHO amongst the agencies mentioned has tried to concentrate on poverty focussed programmes which strengthens national delivery capacity but has recently recognised that actual focus is being lost at the regional and national delivery level.

Currently, UNICEF and World Bank are trying to strengthen national delivery capacity for their programmes and a lot of training and information support accompanies their programme and project activities. UNICEF is making new efforts to strengthen its inter-agency field programmes and now has the largest number of joint programmes of all UN agencies. The World Bank, Population Health

and Nutrition Division is undertaking extensive
health institution and manpower strengthening
support in its health projects as well as being
highly Primary Health Care focussed. At the same
time, partly because of the cuts in IDA
subscriptions, the number of approved Bank and IDA
agriculture and rural development projects are
diminishing (83 in 1981 and 63 in 1984). Also WHO
is in the process of tightening the delivery end of
its own programmes. The real dilemmas that lie
behind these efforts are how to ensure country
programme relevance and delivery strengthening
capability without placing the programmes in the
hands of those who have no interest in seeing them
succeed.

UNDP has been dependent on the developed
countries for funds and the relatively equal
balance of votes in the governing council has
presented scope for the UNDP Secretariat to focus
its programmes at both country and inter-regional
levels. That both types of projects are so widely
spread amongst the sectors is a partial[7]
indication that it has not attempted to strongly
provide such a focus. UNDP's evolving concept of
technical cooperation has recently included not
only the use of its own office of Projects
Execution, rightly or wrongly considered by the
other specialised agencies (and JIU[8]) as
competitive, but also a more passive acceptance of
government use of UNDP funds, albeit with lower
unit costs through government project execution and
national appointed long term and international
short term experts.[9]

Despite the increasing convergence of opinion
by agencies on approaches to be adopted, the effect
on budgets at the country level is not clear. WHO
aims to follow up to find out what is actually
happening; given the budget system of agencies
where poverty focussed or rural development
projects are rarely identified within the budget
headings, this last task will not be easier for WHO
than for the other agencies. ILO has identified
headquarter rural sub-programmes in its 1984/85
budget but without showing the budgetary amounts
for sub-programmes. Within FAO, I have made a rough
estimate that only 13% of the technical budget is
clearly identified for small farm or rural
development support.[10] FAO has made efforts
since the World Conference on Agrarian Reform and
Rural Development (1979), not only within its
organisation, in the strengthening of the Human

Resources, Institutions and Agrarian Reform
Division, and the recent small farm emphasis of the
Investment Centre, but in promoting the interests
of its progeny, the International Fund for
Agricultural Development (IFAD).

There is a big gap in the medium term plans of
agencies in that there is no budgetary weighting
shown to programmes, so that it is not easy to
appreciate from the programme listings where the
overall priority is to be placed. Also, the actual
biennial budgets cannot be analysed in terms of
declared statements of policy focus. For example,
WHO's policy emphasis on 'Health for All'
strategies through Primary Health Care (PHC) cannot
be analyzed in the biennial budgetary allocations,
as PHC is to be seen in all programmes – but
because it cannot be identified, it may, it is
feared, be in very few of them.

The UN Medium Term Plan 1984–1989 has
initially concentrated on focussing within existing
programmes rather than to establish priorities
between programmes. Indeed if a focus exists in the
UN Medium Term Plan, it is more on
industrialisation and energy than on the rural
sector.

The worry is that, despite the formal
processes set up to deal with the long term UN
System wide objectives, the strength of
underlying trends, political focus and greater
public sensitivity to relief than development, the
UN System has reconciled itself to acting as a
social safety net rather than aiming to influence
the causes of development. Even then, the holes in
the net will grow larger as the System cannot keep
pace.

UN agencies have appreciated that, even within
a development and not a relief context, single
sector development programmes unrelated to a wider
policy context can create as many problems as they
solve. Just a few examples will illustrate;
domestic water supplies can only be kept
functioning at a health preserving standard if
local people participate in maintenance and for
this, communities must be technically
knowledgeable, understand the need and be
administratively supported; health care programmes
will grow even more costly if people cannot pay for
food or grow it or know its nutritional content and
for this they must also be administratively
supported. Domestic water boreholes will be used
for cattle leading to over-grazing and unrestrained

74

livestock growth; tree planting and soil erosion prevention programmes (i.e. Nepal foothills or the Ethiopian highlands) do not reduce the mounting pressure on marginal lands from the growing population of the landless. In each case, the problem is inter-sectoral, involves more than one agency in government and the UN System and programmes must be backed by a shift in policy and political will if solutions are to be found. The World Bank, UNEP and a UN Population Conference Expert Group, have called attention[11] to the interaction between deforestation, desertification, agricultural expansion and population growth and migration. Unless these problems are addressed directly, and in the first instance by the coordinated weight at all levels of the UN System, then the outlook is distinctly bleak.

ARE THE REPRESENTATIVE BODIES BLOCKING RURAL POVERTY ORIENTED PROGRAMMES?

There is a question as to whether the representative bodies of the UN System are more responsible than the secretariats for the lack of real progress on UN assisted rural development programmes. By representative bodies is meant the general assemblies and the executive or governing boards of the UN and specialised agencies. For the UN it is the General Assembly, Economic and Social Council (ECOSOC) and their committees; the specialised agencies each use different titles but most have one assembly and one governing board or executive committee.

Public disagreements emerge finally in the general assemblies; where possible, working agreements are made in the governing (and executive) boards. In fact, broad rural development issues have not been a source of disagreement which has spilled over to the general assemblies. It is in the governing boards that the balance of forces needs to be examined. What is found is that the composition of the boards and their constitutional terms of reference may vary between agencies but that in general, there is no consistent blocking of rural programme initiatives. Admittedly, if there had been a sharper policy and programme focus, it is unclear whether blocking would have been more consistent and open. Table 4.1 shows the 1983/84 potential balance of voting within World Bank denominated country groups in selected UN agency governing boards and the UN Committee on

Table 4.1

Balance of Voting by World Bank Country Groups[1]
in the Governing Bodies of the UN System Agencies 1983/4

	World Bank		WHO		FAO		ILO		UNICEF		UNDP		CPC	
	% Countries	% Votes	Votes	%	Votes	%	Votes	%	Votes	%	Votes	%	Votes	%
1. Low Income[2]	27	14	10	35	7	21	21	9	16	12	29	12	25	3	14
2. Lower Middle	31	12	1	4	11	34	34	11	20	6	15	6	13	5	24
3. Upper Middle[3]	17	8	8	29	4	12	12	8	14	6	15	8	17	5	24
4. High oil Exports[4]	3	3	1	4	1	3	3	0	0	1	2	1	2	0	0
5. Eastern Europe	6	–	2	7	2	6	6	3	5	3	7	4	8	2	10
6. Industrialised market	15	63	6	21	8	24	24	25	45	13	32	17	35	6	28
Total	100	100	28	100	33	100	100	56	100	41	100	48	100	21	100

1 Not all countries represented on the governing bodies are in the World Bank list but these have been grouped by separate reference to per capita income statistics; there are 125 countries in the World Bank list.
2 $410 GNP per capita.
3 $1700 GNP per capita.
4 Libya, Saudi Arabia, Kuwait, United Arab Emirates.
5 Government, employers and workers representatives included together.
6 Committee on Programme Coordination.

Programme Coordination. There is considerable
variability of voting strength between agencies
amongst the low, lower middle and upper middle
income groups, which is to be expected as elections
for seats is in mainly regional blocs. Voting power
of the industrialised market economies is
consistently above their strength by numbers (15%
of World Bank countries) but less than their
strength by economic power (63% represented by
voting shares in the World Bank). For rural
development issues, there could be complex actual
or potential voting patterns with some of the low
or lower middle income countries more likely to
vote with industrialised market economies than the
upper middle groups who want higher priority to
industry. The North West country block votes in
ILO, UNDP and UNICEF governing bodies is much above
their share of countries.However voting strength is
more a potential than an actual measure of the
influence of groups, as every attempt is made to
take decisions by concensus rather than votes.
Still the concensus on rural development and
poverty oriented programmes within governing boards
of UN agencies is remarkable and owes very little
to the voting structure of the wider assemblies.
That the concensus exists is more important than
the devious motivations and interests that lie
behind it. However, a judgement on what lies behind
the concensus can be hazarded; the developed
country governments are in favour of poverty
oriented programmes because they consider a) aid
resources being absorbed by those who least need
them b) the wider implications of continued
population growth in developing countries and c)
large scale and modern sector external investment
is best handled by the private sector and
transnational corporations. Developed countries do
not want the commitment to perpetuate their own
agricultural surpluses on a long term basis just to
feed the developing countries, although it may
satisfy some strategical considerations in the
short term.

Although, in developed countries, the civil
servants and aid agencies especially are broadly in
favour of poverty concentrated rural development
programmes, they are not very resistant to less
focussed country requests and do not want to
contain their own sectoral interest groups which
help generate the requests at the country level.
Thus the bilateral aid agencies also frequently end
up with a highly diversified and unfocussed
technical cooperation and aid programme.

Sometimes in hope, the aid agency civil servants turn to the UN System for support but do not find any strong point of coordination from which they can gain strength to help focus their programmes.

The developing country representatives on governing councils are still more ambivalent. They are able to support policies in the UN representative bodies of which they most probably sincerely approve, but when they return home they acquiesce in different priorities, not just in government's own domestic policies, but in the use of the UN System (and bilateral) technical cooperation programmes.

The regional committees of WHO are an interesting example of the hesitation of representatives when they are nearer their own countries. These committees are very reluctant to criticise the WHO budget proposals of fellow member countries. WHO wants country programme relevance by decentralising to the countries and regions but also seeks to have policy focussed country programmes. It is thus currently looking for innovative ways of focussing programmes, ranging from 'in-camera' meetings of regional sub-committees to country and regional programme audits.

The developing country representatives for each agency come mainly from the closest sectoral ministry, i.e., Health (for WHO), Labour (for ILO), Industry (for UNIDO), Planning and Finance (for World Bank), Social Affairs (for UNICEF). The representatives sometimes have their voting instructions prior-coordinated by ministries of planning or foreign affairs, but mainly for political issues, seldom are the programme or broad budgetary questions considered of sufficient importance. Greater focus of policy on poverty oriented programmes has not been an area generally where ministries of foreign affairs or planning have intervened negatively. Influential member countries have sometimes been able to distort the programme balance of the agencies; it is argued below that if the secretariat response had been able to be firmer, there would not have been a programme distortion. These distortions, where they have occurred, have been the result of the highly sensitive and defensive secretariat stance of agencies, which is itself a response to relative agency isolation and weakness.

The question of agency secretariat
responsibility, for the low priority of rural
development within UN policy and programmes can be
examined from four directions, policy and programme
priorities, internal agency focus, coordination of
field programmes and finally a review of the
inter-agency task force on rural development.

DO POLICY COORDINATION MECHANISMS FOR RURAL DEVELOPMENT FUNCTION?

The UN System has made some further progress
towards planning and programming coordination since
the 1978 restructuring exercise[12] but
coordination is still more in form than substance.
The formal structure is that the strategy for the
International Development Decade, covering a ten
year period, leads into a six year period of
detailed medium term plans and bi-annual budgets.
Only the strategy for the International Development
Decade is a System wide exercise. Coordination from
then on is provided by the representative committee
on Programme Coordination (CPC) reporting to ECOSOC
and the secretariat Advisory Committee on
Coordination (ACC) and its sub-committees, the
Consultative Committee on Substantive Questions
(CCSQ) and the task forces on Rural Development and
Long Term Development Objectives. In addition, also
reporting to ECOSOC, is the Joint Inspection Unit
(JIU) that can make independent institutional
evaluations on request.
Whether or not the representative bodies would
be capable of, or want to make, the crucial
inter-agency priority decisions is separate from
the fact that at the moment there is no
institutional means for them to do so. The strategy
for the Third International Development Decade [13]
deals mainly in broad principles and maintains a
balance in sectoral prorities, reflecting in good
part the existing programmes of the agencies. The
general regulations for a common planning and
programme cycle have been agreed by the General
Assembly,[14] but there has been delay in the
detailed planning cycle rules that agencies should
follow and up to now there are separate medium term
plans for each agency, including the UN, but no
System wide programme. The JIU considers[15] the
content of the 'rules' as one of principle because
the secretariat did not appear to want plans
written in terms of major programmes to

open up discussions of objectives and priorities; the 1984-89 UN Medium Term[16] Plan contains only sub-programme analysis and for the main part confirms both the current programmes and the existing UN units which run them.

The CPC and ACC between them have made a number of cross sectoral and cross organisational programme analyses[17]. The various secretariat inter-agency committees such as that on Natural Resources, Water Resources, Steering Committee for the International Drinking Water and Sanitation Decade, have also attempted programme coordination[18]. The JIU has concluded in its review, that no matter how pointed the terms of reference of papers requested in reviews of coordination, the result is usually an uncritical assessment or a "descriptive catalogue" of agency programmes in the area concerned[19]. No programme evaluation really assesses whether a major impact has been made on the problem area or not. The CPC which is a strong representative review body depends on the ACC for papers on coordination matters. The JIU is not designed or staffed to undertake full programme evaluations; it is an institutional review not a programme review body.

It might have been expected that the ACC Task Force on Long Term Development objectives could have monitored demographic, spatial and environmental, along with medium term macro-economic trends to provide feedback to the UN Programme Planning cycle; UNEP and HABITAT are noticeably not participating in meetings. In any case, the Task Force does not see its role as assessing what should be the reaction of the UN System to its deliberations; even the comments on progress of the Third Development Decade strategy were confined to global trends not global UN strategy.

The Consultative Committee on Substantive Questions of the ACC has sponsored a number of joint planning exercises where one agency takes the lead; an early exercise on Primary Health Care has not progressed far as yet, but the experience of this type of lead agency exercise, such as the FAO led Task Force on Rural Development (see Section 8 below) does not suggest that another such exercise may have a greater chance of success.

Coordination of the UN System at the Country Level

At the country level the UNDP Resident

Representative (RRUNDP) is the key person responsible for the UN System; however, neither by their policy nor by their behaviour do all agencies accept this role and sometimes the agency representatives, especially WHO and UNICEF, regard themselves as equal and therefore outside the control of the RRUNDP. In the absence of very firm policy, the ability of a RRUNDP to coordinate activities of agencies depends partly on personality and partly on his influence through the technical cooperation budget of the UNDP Country Programme. The WHO and UNICEF have their own Technical Cooperation budgets which partly explains their ability to take an independent line.

The General Assembly has reiterated a number of times [20] that it wants the Resident Representative UNDP (RRUNDP) to coordinate the UN agencies at the country level. The ACC eventually responded by issuing guidelines,[21] but it was only by the end of 1980 that the designation of 'Resident Coordinators' became operational. Even after that date the impatience of the General Assembly can be felt in the most recent resolutions. The tasks allocated to the Resident Coordinators were overall coordination of country level UN System operational activities, the exercise of team leadership of UN System personnel, and activation of a multidisciplinary dimension to the UN System sectoral programmes. Agency country representatives, when they do not wish to submit to the leadership of the Resident Coordinators, can exploit the fact that the government is ultimately responsible for external coordination; also, the route chosen by agency representatives is frequently through sectoral ministries when the central ministry of planning or foreign affairs responsible for coordination may be unaware of agreements or decisions made.

The absence of both a clear UN System wide policy document which gives a priority for rural development and UNDP guidelines for Resident Coordinators on how to undertake the multidisciplinary dimension of country level UN System programming, certainly inhibits actual field level coordination activities for rural development. There are procedural guidelines for UNDP country programme exercises (to spend the UNDP technical cooperation funds), but these do not insist that country programmes should be consistent with UN System wide policy. In the absence of either a clearly focussed policy guideline within UNDP at the country level or any accepted higher level inter-agency policy, the RRUNDP relies mainly on his style of operation and personality to coordinate the other agencies and produce a fruitful UNDP country programming dialogue with the government.

Sometimes there are regular meetings of the UN System agency representatives within countries called by the RRUNDP (or Resident Coordinators); these may also be interspersed with meetings with the bilateral donors. However, there is no rule about these meetings and although agreements are reached on particular project programming, questions and administrative problems are sorted out, there is no across the board joint programming exercise organised on a regular basis. Again the RRUNDP only has his style and personality to rely on to produce a degreee of internal agency programme consistency.

At the international level of policy formulation, UN System policy is loose and general in its wording and at the national level there are few points of reference. National agency representatives can refer to their own policy documents and regional or headquarter guidelines. The RRUNDP or Resident Coordinator therefore cannot rely on any single document to focus the efforts of the agencies, and from the point of view of coordination, is perhaps over-reticent about his status to remind a national agency representative of his own policy document, even where this was sufficiently widely available that the Resident Coordintor or RRUNDP was aware of it.

Has Joint Programming Worked?

To examine this subject, two important elements were studied. First, what was the role of UNDP, World Bank and also UNEP in using their funds for concentrating agencies into joint programmes? Secondly, how effective has the follow-up to the WCARRD conference been, especially through the work of the UN Advisory Committee on Coordination (ACC) Task Force on Rural Development?

UNDP has policies for inter-regional budget expenditure but these have been so variable that agencies requesting these UNDP funds only perceived them by trial and error; there has certainly not been any consistent attempt to use the inter-regional funds to promote joint agency activities (for example in either rural development or the Water Decade). The policy sections of UNDP have recognised the possibility of promoting inter-agency coordination by its set of Evaluation Studies Such as the one (No. 2 of June 1979) on "Rural Development". At headquarters support levels there have been fewer joint support project activities than at national levels. At the country level there are joint agency activities in rural development but they are also relatively few in number.[22] The UNDP funds a varying but mainly a minority proportion of the specialised agency technical cooperation activities and therefore its coverage would have been small. Its view of the difficulties of coordination were given in the already quoted Evaluation Study of Rural Development.

> "The compartmentalisation between technical line ministries and their relationships to the ministries of planning and finance find a virtual mirror image in the UN System of specialised agencies and their relationships to the UNDP Resident Representative in the field."

Generally now the UNDP shies away from the added difficulty of inter-agency projects.

The current African crisis was a test for the UN System in its ability to produce rapid coordinated results. The appointment of the UNDP Administrator as the UN Secretary-General's representative in charge of the Unit to coordinate the UN System response was an indication of a further attempt to recognise the UNDP's coordinating responsibility. The World Bank commands more funds but its development, rather than emergency, programme for Africa focused the coordinating role perhaps less strongly. The two bodies, to their credit, moved to work together in an impressive manner. The major donor aid agencies cooperated in an exemplary fashion during the crisis and even went so far as to agree to"advocate" in the governing bodies of international agencies a similarly responsive attitude by these agencies.[23]

The UNDP formed with the UNFPA, the WFP and UNICEF a Joint Consultative Group on Policy in the areas of health and nutrition. The fear is that real coordination will only result from a relief crisis and where it is also absolutely essential, in long term technical cooperation policy and programmes, the motivation given by the emergency in Africa will soon evaporate.

UNEP has been effective in using its funds to produce research studies with other agencies on some of the crucial inter-sectoral development and environment linkages. The UNESCO "Man and the Biosphere Programme" supported by UNEP has made significant contributions. The link back through inter-agency support and country level activities to provide remedies is missing and it is certainly too much to expect that UNEP on its own could promote these activities.

The coordinating machinery confirmed by the 1979 WCARRD Conference was the Inter-Agency Task Force on Rural Development and the lead role was given to the FAO. The FAO was the follow-up on the UN System programme of action in monitoring and evaluation, information dissemination, enhanced technical assistance and resource mobilisation. A lot of effort has gone into developing monitoring and evaluation indicators, establishing and strengthening the Regional Rural Development Centres and inter-governmental consultations. At the country level effort has also gone into inter-agency joint policy review missions and attempts to set up national governmental and UN agency working coordinating committees. The ACC Inter-Agency Task Force on Rural Development was in existence before WCARRD and had an initial aim of joint agency planning.[24] After WCARRD the Task Force also considered attempting cross organisational programme analysis; this never really became an effective activity. The Task Force was reappraised by ACC and drew up a work programme with specific outputs of direct and immediate use to governments. The work decided upon was mainly on monitoring, evaluation and an attempt to develop some joint activities in people's participation.

A preliminary overview of the work of the Task Force leads to the following conclusions:

1. the monitoring and evaluation techniques devised are still in dissemination stage so that no significant results have appeared to feed back to country policy response;
2. no effective mechanism is available to feed back the result of monitoring and evaluation to national policy;
3. the country policy review reports combine policy and broad programme recommendations but

as policy dialogue and follow up mechanisms
with government by the UN System from the
WCARRD mechanisms are weak, the reports are
put on the shelf;

4.	there is more problem of joint agency
identification and detailed programming of
projects than of implementation once they are
agreed;

5.	little progress has been made on strengthening
either national or UN country coordinating
mechanisms;

6.	the Regional Rural Development Centres have
been starved of resources by countries and
some are barely operative;

7.	Regional inter-agency consultations that have
no decisions to take or policy papers to agree
produce few concrete results.

TOWARDS MORE EFFECTIVE COORDINATION

A Summary of Current Coordination Difficulties

A summary of the concerns exposed in the previous
sections will help to put in perspective the
reforms proposed:

1.	high level overviews provided by the ACC and
DIESA reports either are not firm enough on
focussing priorities or lack recommendations;

2.	the concept of rural development is still
considered too narrow for it to be seen to
provide priority in an overview of UN System
wide development policy;

3.	there is no effective mechanism of UN System
wide medium term programming or joint
programming which would be able to support
country multi-sectoral rural development;

4.	the General Assembly and ECOSOC are swamped
with material and are in no position at the
moment to assert development priorities
without strong secretariat support; joint
forums of the governing bodies of agencies are
rare (the joint UNICEF/WHO Committee on Health
Policy is an exception).

5.	the concept of lead agency is inadequate to
provide agency coordination and significant
budget contributions;

6.	the UNDP country programme is not fully
effective in supporting the RRUNDP in his role
as Resident Coordinator of UN System
programmes at the country level;

7.   no flexible and easy to operate guidelines
     exist for the RRUNDP and Resident Coordinators
     to prepare their mandate of multidisciplinary
     programmes (especially for rural development);
8.   the concept of technical cooperation which
     supports the strengthening of national
     infrastructures working for UN System policies
     is still weakly defined and accepted within
     the System.

Too Many Problems in an Uncontrolled Multi-agency System

It was well appreciated and intentional that when
the question of rural development was raised the
issue of the development role of the UN and the
operational agencies would be opened up. Is there
any way to make the existing System work
fundamentally better or are radical changes in the
System necessary to produce an effective operation?
     One suggestion resulting from the examination
of reports of meetings of the representative bodies
of the UN System is that there is near unanimity
(at least at headquarters levels), on the need for
a poverty oriented focus and also for a
strengthened and coordinated UN Programme to
achieve it. The benefits of heterogeneity and
agency independence and proliferation is more a
secretariat sponsored idea aided by the special
interests within sectoral ministries. There is a
relation between countries' fear of a monolithic UN
System wide planning structure and the unresponsive
nature of UN agency secretariats; the more
heterogeneous the System, the more secretariats are
able to appeal to special sectoral interests and to
juggle secretariat country quotas and senior
appointments. Political battles there will be,
within a stronger federal structure, but the issues
can be contained at the higher levels of policy.

Can the United Nations Coordinate with or Control the World Bank Group?

There is so much scope for improved efficiency
within the relation between the UN and the 'one
country one vote' specialised agencies that the
issue of how to integrate the World Bank and IFAD
(with weighted voting) can temporarily be put to
one side; some other suggested experiments (as in
Chapter 3) to create a high level policy forum
comprising the two types of voting structures,

within the area of global economic management may
assist in showing how an integration might be made.
It can also be appreciated from the review made
here how much more balanced is the voting structure
of executive bodies as distinct from the wider
assemblies of the specialised agencies. Only where
the political battle raises fundamental issues will
it be referred to the specialised agency main
assembly without the executive body full
concurrence. Even appreciating this factor will not
be enough to ensure World Bank agreement to take
part in all the recommended reforms but it will be
enough if the Bank stays with the ACC as it assumes
stronger coordinating functions. The issue of how
much priority for rural development may be disputed
without some 'global contract' on trade and
finance, but such trade-offs can be pushed off to a
higher level forum. As long as there was such a
forum which could act as a safety valve for major
political issues of this kind, the existing UN
System development institutions can be made to
function, albeit with some fundamental changes in
policy and procedure as indicated below.

A United Nations System Wide Planning Cycle

A great deal of effort has been devoted by the UN
to strengthening its own planning cycle; the
emphasis has not been misplaced. Once a coherent
planning cycle is in place for the UN there would
be a case for strengthening the UN General Assembly
responsibility also for the specialised agency
medium term plans.
        Within the UN, the whole emphasis should be on
providing a small tight overview, policy planning
and coordinating group to service not only its own
substantive development activities (i.e. UNEP,
UNIDO), but also the inter-agency programming and
coordinating committees. If this was accepted as
the principal role of the Director General for
Development, there would be scope for substantially
reducing many unrelated sub-programmes. This
recommendation reinforces those of the JIU to
present policy objectives first in medium term
plans rather than sub-programmes, and encourage the
representative bodies to choose priorities.
        The Department for Development can make
multidisciplinary planning and programming its own
special function to provide a counter weight to the
specialised agencies purely sectoral interests. The
expertise in joint planning can service the ACC/CPC

Coordinating Committees as well as the committees of ECOSOC and the general assembly.

The links between the UN System wide policy setting and coordinating role under the Director-General for Development and the policy role of UNDP greatly requires strenthening. UNDP should take its policy from the General Assembly through the Director-General for Development, the UNDP Council confining itself to the raising and administration of funds at the country level. If in the end the answer to the question of who coordinates the UN System development work is some combination of the governing bodies of the World Bank/IMF group and the UN, then UNDP cannot itself expect ultimately to assume this role, even with its Resident Representatives as UN country level coordinators. The tight group of UN secretariat working to the General Assembly committees must have the System wide secretariat policy and coordinating power. One innovation would be to transfer the global and inter-regional programmes function from UNDP to the Director-General for Development and the CPC, which would imply that executive agreement could be reached with the contributory governments that these funds should be transferred. This should not therefore be attempted until the credibility of the UN secretariat coordinating role was demonstrably further strengthened internally.

Joint Programming as Role for the Regional Commissions

The usefulness of the Regional Economic Commissions in development work could be greatly enhanced if they could be explicitly organised on multisectoral programme lines, rather than follow the sector lines of the government ministries and specialised agencies. Inter-regional programme funds can be specifically directed through them to put together the inter-agency teams which conduct the joint planning, programming, technical cooperation for demonstration and replication projects, and programme audits. These are formidable tasks and would amply justify the continued existence of the Regional Commissions.

Coordination through Medium Term Plans

The mid-decade review of the strategy for the Third International Development Decade would present an

opportunity that could be followed up by the
secretariat to present a major new policy paper.
The kind of strategy paper that is required is, in
addition to a brief review of the processes of UN
programme coordination and the national strategies
at country level, to present a detailed statement
of the policy priorities at country level for UN
System agencies and the required programmes of
support at central or regional offices. Medium term
plans should also be given these terms of
reference; bi-annual budgets following the agency
medium term plans can have their headquarters and
regional support programmes closely monitored by
executive or governing bodies, but country
programmes can only be effectively monitored by
periodic audits or evaluations; this has certainly
been the experience of WHO[25]. UN System wide
coordination can be effected through a combination
of medium term plans and country level programme
evaluations or audits. the emphasis given by the
JIU reports is therefore precisely targetted[26];
they have made recommendations to strengthen both
these areas of activity. The power to enforce
coordination once agency medium term plans or
country audits were presented could come from three
possible sources, the budget, control of the
secretariat from within, or control from the
representative bodies. All three will be necessary
eventually.

Coordination through Budgets, Secretariat Line Control and through Agency Representative Bodies

To prevent a bureacratic tangle, it is not
desirable to have a centralised budget for all
agencies. The need for coordination is covered by
control of medium term plans and country audits;
however, it is essential to have some quantitative
priorities included in the medium term plans. It is
not sufficient to state objectives and programme
titles and broad content in medium term plans if
the weighting between them is not also indicated.
The weighting as well as the content should be
mandatory for the bi-annual budgets unless a waiver
is requested and received.

Coordination would be greatly strengthened if
the secretariat of the agencies, starting with the
executive heads, were directly responsible to the
Secretary-General of the United Nations and not to
their governing boards and individual assemblies.
This is the biggest single contribution that could

be made for effective coordination given that a great deal of the responsibility for lack of progress can be ascribed to the independence of agency secretariats. The constitutional position is such that this step cannot be considered to be immediately feasible unless preceded by significant moves to strengthen the control by the representative bodies over the coordination function.

The constraints acting against coordination within the secretariats could be greatly reduced by effectively bringing together the governing bodies of the operational agencies with, for example, either the officers of the Fifth Committee of the General Assembly or the Committee on Programme Coordination. There could be two sorts of meeting; the first is a representative meeting of the chairmen and one other from the governing bodies of the specialised agencies (the second member could come from the specialised agency programme committees) meeting with the Fifth Committee (called chairmen meeting). The second is a meeting of the full programme committee of each agency with the CPC to discuss the agency Medium Term Plan and plan evaluation (Programme Committees meeting). Each would meet formally twice only every six years (with a preparatory and substantive meeting) but there could be more ad hoc informal meetings as required. The chairmen's meeting would discuss a draft evaluation of the previous strategy and a proposal for the next medium term period. The Programme Committees would meet in turn with the CPC to discuss an evaluation of their own previous Medium Term Plan and the draft for the next one. The rights of review and amendment to the specialised agency Medium Term Plans of the General Assembly would grow from precedent without any change in the specialised agency constitutions unless these were proposed. The initial effect would be to build up a new channel of both informal and formal dialogue for the preparation of UN System wide programme policy and agency Medium Term Plans in which the representatives of the governing bodies were the leading actors. Country governments would feel more in control but the spread of countries as a result of the method of representation could preserve the international flavour. In addition, agency secretariats would be more constrained to cooperate in decisions agreed by their governing bodies and their programme committees.

90

Any changes recommended in the work of the CPC and ACC to encourage joint agency planning and programming exercises would have a chance of being realised if the governing bodies become more directly involved. If the recommendations are not implemented there will be as little chance of success in the future as there was in the past. The ACC has recently been able to undertake various cross-sectoral and organisational overviews (human settlement, marine); lead agency run inter-organisational exercises (rural development, primary health care) have replaced joint planning. A programme of joint planning and programming should be tried again and exercises could be proposed by the UN Secretariat for ACC in readiness for the first preparatory Chairmen's meeting. These would suggest country support and demonstration activities and country joint planning and programming guidelines. Rural development joint planning would embrace both primary health care and other rural based non-agricultural programmes. In addition, the UN secretariat could propose a new strategy of technical cooperation at the country level which allows field staff to take a more positive line with those who are working for agreed policies.

A NEW STRATEGY OF TECHNICAL COOPERATION

RRUNDP to Interpret United Nations System Policy at the Country Level

If Resident UN System Coordinators (or RRUNDP) were to develop some resistance to country pressures unfavourable to agreed UN System programme policy or were in fact able to exert a pressure towards it, a whole new strategy of technical cooperation would be required. This would allow technical cooperation to support those within and outside government who were working for rural development. Although sensitive to country needs, because of the strong country based programming mechanism for allocating UN money, the new strategy would still entail a real dialogue, rather than just acting as a postbox for not always equally well directed country demands.

Not only will many donors who contribute to such programmes become more satisfied about UN's competence to administer them more effectively but there is likely to be a firmer response from government offices and ministries once they obtain

a more focussed and consistent support. The
strategy will precede country audits and
evaluations preventing them from showing too
negative a position.
The hinge in the mechanism at the country
level is the UN System Resident Coordinator to whom
support must come from headquarters and regions and
from whom support will go out to all the field
staff for whom he will be responsible. Continuous
dialogue at the highest levels in the System may be
required to overcome individual country resistance
to the wider role of Country Coordinators and the
new strategy of technical cooperation. However
subtle the mixture of positive and negative
incentives to reach initial acceptance by each
country of the Resident Coordinator's role, as the
resolutions suggested which established them,
nothing will be achieved without government support
in principle. Governments are ultimately
responsible for coordination of their external
assistance and therefore for the presence of the
Resident Coordinator. Although the ultimate
sanction of the UN to withdraw some part of its
activities (and those of combined donors) is
matched by the ultimate sanction of government to
disallow the presence of a Resident Coordinator,
there will be many gradations between for
differences to be settled. Support will be sought
and can be expected from the coordinating
ministries and office of the President, and it will
be to these offices the Resident Coordinators will
turn to sustain themselves against the inevitable
pressures of their new role. To support the
Resident Coordinators further, there might be:

1. a clear statement of UN System policies and
   programme priorities can be drafted with each
   country by an inter-agency/government team;
2. joint inter-agency/government programming
   exercises where UN System funds are to be
   committed;
3. a regular cycle and calendar of dialogue
   between government, other country
   representatives and UN to interpret UN System
   and agency priorities into a UN country
   support programme.

Support from Country Coordination Ministries

One innovation in the regular cycle of UN
System/government dialogue would be for each

country to have a high level dialogue to produce
the policy statement of 1 above every four to six
years. For example, the Minister for Planning and
other ministers would meet with the Regional
Administrator UNDP and other Regional Directors. To
guide them, a paper would be prepared by the
Ministry of Planning, DIESA and World Bank. Part of
the policy statement would include an estimate of
the System wide funds being sought and the agency
shares; a review of policies and System programmes
for the period past and in progress would also be
summarised. The UNDP and the World Bank have gone
part of the way along this road in its experimental
technical cooperation planning exercise with the
Government of Somalia in 1984:

> "The forward looking assessment exercise
> focussed on analysing and identifying priority
> requirements within the broad framework of
> the governments plans and objectives. Drawing
> extensively on the experience and knowledge of
> other aid partners, the assessment has also
> led to several important conclusions about the
> more effective use of national personnel and
> technical assistance."[27]

Any country detailed programming and joint
agency/government project programming can then be
guided by this document. It will also back up the
Resident Coordinator in his day-to-day work with
government and the specialised agency
representatives.

Country System Wide Programming

The second innovation in the planning cycle with
government would be country level system wide
programming of which the UNDP Country Programme
would be only a part. At the moment there is little
incentive to undertake within the UNDP/IPF any
"Programme budgeting"[28] or joint
agency/government programmes. With the inter-agency
technical cooperation strategy, System wide Medium
Term Planning, and programme budgeting, the
incentive increases. Inter-sectoral planning will
not only become a meaningful exercise for agencies
but also perhaps, for the first time, for some
countries.

SUMMARY

The existing development agencies of the UN System could be made to function more effectively in rural development without radical restructuring. The initiative would have to be taken by the Fifth Committee of the General Assembly and the Committee on Programme Coordination in active dialogue with the executive bodies of agencies. No one has the incentive to recommend the reforms amongst the agency secretariats, not even the UN Secretariat, which may gain in stature but lose in numbers, from a rationalisation and clearer policy focus.

Coordination of the UN System at headquarters and regional levels, on the one hand and at country levels on the other, would allow the more wide ranging concept of rural development (of strengthening national delivery capacity, as against discrete rural programmes) to be adopted with a stronger chance of success. WHO, for example, which has acknowledged its difficulty in focussing its country programmes after having succeeded at global levels, would gain strength from common system wide country cooperation programmes.

The wider concept of rural development should be an even more important component in the UN strategy for development than it is at the moment. The inability of the System to coordinate effectively partly explains this lack of focus. Therefore, improved UN System coordination and more effective rural development support are mutually reinforcing. The greater concentration on rural development will not eliminate the huge remedial programmes such as those for Africa, but may gradually reduce the disproportionate effort that currently goes into them relative to the more permanent development programmes.

Notes to Chapter 4.

1. UNDP - "Evaluation Study No.2 of Rural Development", June 1979.
2. For the 36 least developed countries the figure is 33%. The figures for 1982 from the 1984 OECD "Geographical Distribution of Financial Flows to Developing countries".
3. World Watch Institute -"State of the World 1986", W.W. Norton and Penguin Books, Ontario, 1986.

4. UNEP -"The State of the Environment
    1972-1982",Nairobi,1982.
        -"The State of the Environment
    1985",Nairobi, 1984.
5. A question much enlightened by the work of
    Prof. A.K. Sen - "Poverty and Famines",
    Oxford, Clarendon Press, 1981.
6. "Rural Communities in the Third World are not
    homogenious entities ... Under these
    circumstances any meaningful approach that
    will not benefit the rich at the expense of
    the poor must be a political approach. In some
    countries the political space° exists for
    such an approach. In others the political
    space° needs to be created or even a crack can
    be widened." - Pona Wignaraja, "Entry Points
    in Innovative Approaches to Rural
    Development", in Society for International
    Development - "Development : Seeds of Change,
    Village Global Order", 1984, No. 2.
7. I made an analysis of Water Decade projects
    from the UNDP 1983 Catalogue of Projects.
    Those Water Decade Projects with rural or
    urban poor, health or community participation
    elements were 37% of the number of projects
    and 35% of their total value. It would have
    been thought from UNDP Water Decade literature
    that a much higher proportion would have been
    focussed to poverty reduction areas.
8. JIU report (A/39/80)
9. DP/1984/SR.15 June 1984, Governing Council
    UNDP, Para. 14.
10. The 13% includes FAO budget classifications
    Chapter 2.15 Rural Development, 2.16,
    Nutrition, 2.34 Forestry for rural development
    and 20% of 4 technical cooperation; the total
    denominator for the percentage excludes
    chapter 1, headquarter overheads.
11. World Bank - "World Development Report 1984".
    (New York), Oxford University Press, p.p.
    94-96;
    UNEP - "The State of the Environment 1984",
    Nairobi (ISBN 92807 1082 6) p.p. 28-31.
    UN - "Population, Resources, Environment and
    Development", Population Studies No. 90. New
    York, 1984, pp. 28-29.
12. See Report of the Ad Hoc Committee on the
    Restructuring of the Economic and Social
    Sectors of the United Nations System. Official
    Records of the General Assembly, Thirty-Second
    Session; Supplement No. 34A (A/32/34), 1978

13. General Assembly: Thirty-fifth Session: Supplement No. 48 (A35/48); Annex to Resolution 35/36; Pp. 106-120. 1981.
14. By Resolution 37/234 of 21 December 1982.
15. Second Report on the Elaboration of Regulations for the Planning, Programme and Evaluation Cycle of the United Nations General Assembly, Thirty-eighth Session A/38/160(JIU/REP/83/6) page 4.1
16. Medium Term Plan For the Period 1984-1989, General Assembly, Thirty-Seventh Session: Supplement No. 6. (A/37/6) 1983.
17. For a list of references see the JIU - "Reporting to the Economic and Social Council" (JIU/REP/84/7) Maurice Bertrand, Geneva 1984.
18. Without much success as is recorded in "Adequate Supply of Safe Water and Basic Sanitation in Relation to the Goal of Health For all and Primary Health Care: Review and Evaluation", WHO EB75/PC/WP/2 20 September 1984, para. 80.
19. JIU/REP/84/7 para. 31.
20. By Resolutions 32/197, 34/213, 37/226
21. Annex to Annual Report of the ACC to ECOSOC in 1979, E(1919/34) add.1, Rev.1
22. From a perusal of the Compendium of Ongoing UNDP Country Projects
23. UNDP-"Policy Review: Coordination of Technical Cooperation at the Country Level and Examination of the Steps Taken by the UNDP to Strengthen Coordination in Practice"; Annual Report of the Administrator for 1984, DP/1985/4,para. 65-67.
24. Report of the Committee on Programme Coordination (CPC) 24th Session Official Records (38 (A/39/38) New York 1984.
25. Programme and Budget 1986-1987, Introduction.
26. Ibid. JIU/REP/83/6 and JIU/REP/84/7
27. UNDP-"Policy Review: Coordination of Technical Cooperation at the Country Level and Examination of the Steps Taken by the UNDP to Strengthen Coordination in Practice"; Annual Report of the Administrator for 1984, DP/1985/4, page 17, para 60.
28. Showing the budget contributions of each agency going towards a specified common programme.

Chapter Five

PROBLEM AREA THREE: THIRD WORLD COLLECTIVE SECURITY
AND DISARMAMENT

BACKGROUND

Is it really impossible to make changes in the
working of the Security Council so that it can
carry out its mandate (under Chapter VII of the
United Nations Charter)? If Maurice Bertrand is
right,[1] that it is impossible to make changes in
the working of the Security Council, then his way
forward to peace and security through economic and
social development may be too long and because of
insecurity, we may never arrive. The
Secretary-General has given in his 40th Anniversary
address to the General Assembly, the highest
priority to peace and security issues. There are
still paths to explore.
     The link between disarmament and security is
clear; countries that are, or even just feel, more
secure will be prepared to reduce their defence
efforts, especially as resource claims from
development and social welfare are also pressing
hard.
     Although the Charter authors had not
appreciated[2] the impact of nuclear arms, which
would prohibit the possiblity of collective
enforcement against a nuclear weapons state, or the
lack of cohesion of the permanent
members, they were responsible for the added
ingredient of the Security Council veto. This
ingredient although representative of power
realities (the growing power of the Third World
Group on the Security Council only reinforcing this
conclusion) has been a particularly harsh and
intractable institutional device, not allowing for
any substantive development.
     Despite this pessimistic background it is
still worth questioning whether there is a possible

way forward through collective security in the
Third World. There are many arguments that even
this channel is likely to prove impassable:
arbitrary ex-colonial boundaries, unequal
development, a strong propensity to military
regimes has created fragility and insecurity.[3]
Developing countries in 1980 made up 16.1% of world
military expenditure relative to 3.3% in 1955.[4]
Third World conflicts have been so further tangled
by super power involvement that no area of the
world is free of their competition[5] and fears
have been expressed[6] that there are gains to be
made by the superpowers in Third World
destabilisation. Especially since the oil price
rises of 1972/73, the uncontrolled conventional
arms race amongst the Third World has been
paralleled by a general reluctance to discuss
conventional arms control in the UN.[7]
    The more optimistic signs are that Third World
countries arms purchases have been declining over
the last few years; economic pressures and arms
satiation have reduced the demand. The
intractability of certain Third World disputes in
Iran/Iraq, Lebanon, Afghanistan, Al-Salvador,
Angola, Chad, has brought an air of stalemate to
the superpower rivalry. Although the Third World
has refused to accept conventional disarmament
before nuclear weapons are abolished, they have
continued to press in the General Assembly for
collective security; given their fragility, it is
reasonable to request security before disarmament.
The permanent nuclear members of the Security
Council are, despite the non-proliferation treaty,
sufficiently worried about more states becoming
nuclear, as well as international terrorism arising
from Third World disputes (which may eventually
have nuclear implications), that they may put a new
gloss on the imperatives of Third World collective
security.
    The non-aligned have become a major force in
the Security Council because they have acted
consistently as a group[8]. China as a permanent
member of the Security Council has played a highly
independent role. If the possibility of a positive
role in the Security Council opened up, the
pressure to switch the Third World positive
contribution from the Security Council to the
General Assembly would be reduced.
    Third World collective Security under the
aegis of the Security Council, may inhibit not only
external 'aggression' but also slow down the

process of internal political change. For example, if collective security halts inter-state 'aggression', it is doubtful whether it can also put parallel restraints on régimes under internal pressure from seeking outside assistance from friendly governments. What then would be the impact of a tight link between collective security and disarmament?

The 10th Special Session on Disarmament of the General Assembly set up an expert study group on the subject of disarmament and security which reported to the follow-up 12th Special Session. The expert study group covered the principles but did not venture an opinion as to the details of how the Charter Collective Security activities could be made more effective.[9] It was the report of the Independent Commission on Disarmament[10] under the chairmanship of Olaf Palme that did venture into some detail. The Olaf Palme report was available to the 12th Special Session on Disarmament but as this assembly could not reach agreements on any issue, the report was not carried any furthur forward.[11]

The Olaf Palme Commission report suggested that Security Council decided enforcement measures and strengthened peace-keeping activities could be used to prevent Third World border disputes. Although less contentious for the permanent members of the Security Council than either General Assembly channels or Collective Security applied to nuclear powers, it may be a precedent they may not wish to have accepted. Also the Third World would want to know both, they were not succumbing to First or Second World dominance, by other means; nor inviting interference in their internal affairs. The strong relationship between internal and external security also complicates the issues[12] more than the Palme Commission was prepared to admit.

This chapter explores the arguments behind the Olaf Palme suggestion, especially concentrating on the changes which might be envisaged in Security Council procedures to carry out collective security operations in the Third World, recognising the problems outlined in the previous paragraph. It examines the counter pressures to put more peace and security responsibilities on the General Assembly and finally proposes a Commission of the Security Council to unite currently disparate United Nations functions, of peace and security, information gathering, peaceful settlement of disputes, enforcement operations and (conventional forces) disarmament.

PEACE AND SECURITY IN THE UN UNDER THE CHARTER: PAST PROBLEMS AND RECENT DEVELOPMENTS

The impasse in the Security Council on major issues has recently grown even more serious. Prior to the formalised relationship of the non-aligned countries on the Security Council early in 1979, only the permanent members could block decision by veto; since that time the non-aligned countries have developed the capacity to block decision also by their relatively coherent policies and sub-group meetings.[13]

The use by the Security Council of informal processes and closed sessions combined with a Secretariat that has not the capacity or the close relationship with the Council to produce enough and timely papers to act as an objective and partial counterweight has produced what Urquhart has called an "increasingly expedient and evasive approach to world problems".[14]

Although the Charter is clear about enforcement actions being reserved for the Security Council, the inability to make significant progress in the Security Council has seen frequent attempts by the General Assembly to play a more dominant role.

Powers of the General Assembly in Peace and Security Matters

The General Assembly is empowered to discuss and recommend measures on peace and security matters by the United Nations Charter, but only with the agreement of states where domestic jurisdiction would otherwise be infringed. Only the Security Council can go beyond these limits.

"Not only could the Assembly discuss such problems (questions or situations threatening peace and security), but it could also present appropriate recommendations to the Council. What the Assembly could not do was to adopt decisions the implementation of which required the taking of actions involving the use of force. That right under the Charter belonged exclusively to the Security Council".[15]

Article 10 of the Charter gives the General

Assembly powers to discuss and recommend to its members on any matter within the scope of the Charter. The scope of the Charter is limited (under Chapter 1, article 2, para.7) to matters outside the domestic jurisdiction of states unless with their agreement; action under Chapter VII dealing with enforcement are specifically excluded from this limitation. Article 11 says:

> "Any such question on which action is necessary shall be referred to the Security Council by the General Assembly either before or after discussion".

Article 14 states that the General Assembly can make recommended measures for the peaceful adjustment of disputes. The distinction between "recommended measures" able to be put forward to UN members by the General Assembly and enforcement "actions" solely available to the Security Council was narrowed by the Uniting for Peace Resolution 337(V) of 3 November 1950.

The Uniting for Peace Resolution allowed the General Assembly to take up international peace and security issues and organise peace-keeping forces. The conformity of the resolution to the Charter depends on the judgement that "recommended measures" in article 14 implies that the General Assembly can "take some kind of action". This was so argued by the International Court of Justice (ICJ),[16] but the judgement was questioned by dissenting opinions[17]. Conformity with the Charter, even allowing the validity of the ICJ ruling, still depends on a very fine distinction, between peace-keeping forces involving non-coercive armed action (by agreement with the parties), open to the General Assembly and coercive action against one or more states, open to the Security Council. Peace keeping forces have turned the legal necessity into a virtue because by not shooting except in self defence, peace-keeping forces command a respect which allows them to do more with smaller resources; nevertheless, the distinction in practice is still a fine one.

The vote in the Security Council which passes a problem to the General Assembly to deal with under the Uniting for Peace Resolution[18] gives added legal basis to the Resolution because it is an admittance that the Security Council cannot carry out its primary responsibility under the Charter. The fact that such a vote goes through without veto as a procedural question (Charter, article 27.2) is a legal niceity which in the past caused real political problems. Despite the fact that both superpowers have had the weapon used against themselves, the legal point that a way around the Charter was available which had not received the consent of all the parties greatly concerned the Soviet Union up to very recently. This viewpoint was reiterated in a recent 1985 UNIDIR publication:[19]

> "Under the Charter of the United Nations, the investigation of any disputes and situations the continuance of which is likely to endanger the maintenance of international peace and security and the taking of decisions and action relating to such disputes and situations are within the competence of the Security Council alone. To no other organ of the United Nations does the Charter assign such a function. Consequently, attempts to broaden the powers of the General Assembly, the International Court and the Secretary-General to the detriment of the corresponding powers of the Security Council cannot be described as anything other than anti-constitutional, 'anti-Charter'."

Since 1975, the Security Council veto has been used more by the U.S. than the Soviet Union. R.L. Jackson reports that from 1946-1982, of the 187 vetos, 112 were Soviet and 35 U.S.; from 1975-182, the U.S. cast 29 vetos and the Soviet Union only 4. The Soviet Union has become increasingly sensitive to the opinion, and willing to dialogue with, the non-aligned group on the Security Council.[20] However as McWhinney writes, the two superpowers combined weight on the issue is formidable:

> "If one joins the Soviet Union's historical and doctrinally based restrictive, limiting approach to the United Nations and international organisations generally, and to the office of Secretary-General in particular, the United States attempt in the early 1980s to translate domestic 'Reagonomics' and budget paring to the international arena and its increasing conservatism and timorousness in the face of the robust Third World majority in the General Assembly, one has an unholy alliance of formidable dimensions".[21]

A new flexibility on the part of the Soviet Union and some additional steps towards "peaceful coexistence" from the United States could as rapidly shift the impasse and alter the perceived usefulness of some at least of the UN political forums. If there is a new tide, can a boat be found to catch it?

Appeals by the Secretary-General and Response of the General Assembly and Security Council

The Secretary-General has attempted to force the issue of the limited actual role of the Security Council in international peace and security in relation to the potential within the United Nations Charter.

> "The Security Council, the primary organ of the United Nations for the maintenance of international peace and security, all too often finds itself unable to take decisive action to resolve international conflicts and its resolutions are increasingly defied or ignored by those that feel themselves strong enough to do so. Too frequently the Council seems powerless to generate the support and influence to ensure that its decisions are respected, even when these are taken unanimously. Thus the process of peaceful settlement of dispute prescribed in the Charter is often brushed aside."[22]

The result of the Secretary-General's comments has been to stimulate both discussion in the Security Council, as well as a counter response in committees of the General Assembly. No outcome has generated sufficient pressure for any real change to be perceived.

The Security Council has met a number of times, mostly in private, specifically to review the Secretary-General's comments. Consideration was given to various proposals, setting up subsidiary structures (under Charter Article 29), measures to prevent the aggravation of disputes, measures to facilitate prompt action, more effective information gathering for the Council, the holding of periodic meetings (as distinct from meetings requested by UN members); to strengthen peace-keeping operations and activate The Military Staff Committee and other innovative ideas to

revitalise the concept of collective security. By
the time of the 39th General Assembly the Council
was still deliberating in private on a continuing
basis.[23] The Secretary-General has commented in
all three reports, since the one quoted, on his
disappointment that there have been no developments
and his hope that there will be by 1986 which is
the International Year of Peace. The detailed
points made by the Secretary-General are:

- the unwillingness of the Council to take
  seriously the collective Security "sterner
  measures" provisions of the Charter;
- the impact of the unanimity (veto rule);
- the need for prior work by the Council to
  anticipate disputes and to intervene at an
  early junction;
- to prepare itself with fact-finding and
  information;
- hold periodic meetings for over-view reports
  and planning;
- inability to follow up resolutions made and
  acceptance of resolutions as a substitute for
  action;
- the use of the Council as a public podium.

Apart from a strong paper by the Nordic group
supporting[24] the Secretary-General's position,
the response of the General Assembly has been
discordant and uncoordinated. Unconnected
resolutions have been put forward as a result of,
follow up to the disarmament special sessions,[25]
resolutions from the First Committee,[26] and
reports of the Special Charter Committee.[27] In
the debate within the First Committee on draft
resolutions to set up a permanent "Ad Hoc
Committee" to explore ways and means of
implementing the Charter provision on collective
security, some non-aligned members expressed the
view, "we are aware that powerful groups are
opposed to the action and are determined even now
to do every thing possible to frustrate it."[28]
All the permanent members of the Security Council
excepting for China voted against the resolution to
establish this permanent committee.[29] The same
frustrations have also blocked the Charter
Committee and the Special Committee on Peace
Keeping in producing guidelines, the first on
procedures for good offices, mediation and
conciliation (which may eventuate)[30] and the
second on all aspects of peace-keeping forces

(which will most probably not).31 Similar
resolutions from different forums coming forward
uncoordinated to the General Assembly allow the
issues to go by default. Only unanimous resolutions
are really treated seriously in the General
Assembly and its Committees.

Most of the suggestions to reform the Security
Council involve some form of limiting the strength
of the veto; either the Council should have
membership, or members with veto power, extended
or, the category of "procedural matters" to which
the veto power does not apply should be increased
or, gentleman's agreements could be entered into
not to use the veto on particular kinds of issue.
These procedures would help decisions to be made
but in no way increase the chance of effective
resolution of conflicts. However, unfair and
non-representative of world changing balance of
forces is the Security Council, without a more
effective disputes settlement procedure in sight,
neither arbitration procedures nor collective
security enforcement, there is not likely to be any
surrender of power made by the existing permanent
members of the Security Council.

POLITICAL REALITIES AND POSSIBLE OUTCOMES

Security Council or General Assembly

Acknowledging that procedural and institutional
reforms cannot help and probably will not be
successfully implemented if the political will is
not there32 should not be allowed to dominate all
reform efforts. Institutional reforms have to be
ready and agreed for the moment when political
realities fall into place. For example, on each
occasion that peace-keeping forces have been
established, the political pressures have
frequently been sufficient to overcome
constitutional niceities.

It is to be expected that countries will bring
their special interests to the United Nations and
when not able to make their voice heard there, will
use all available means outside. More or less
democratic organisations can always either wait for
the auspicious moment, or at the best, leading
voices with the help of the Secretariat can lever
the political interests into a favourable
alignment. However the unanimity rule in the
Security Council is really rather a special
procedure as it gives any permanent member the

right to block all movement. The increased
cohesiveness of the non-aligned within the Security
Council combined with the unanimity rule for
permanent members implies that there is just a
further force for blocking any movement. Whatever
the power politics and constitutional justification
for change, there have been no signs, in fact the
opposite, that the permanent members would
sacrifice any of their prerogatives; without all
their signatures change is impossible.

Even though the Soviet Union has since the
middle 1970s not had so much recourse to the veto,
it still feels strongly about the alternative
pathway of using the General Assembly and pushing
the "Uniting for Peace Resolution" to the outer
edges of its practicality. In the same way that the
other permanent members supporting the 'Uniting for
Peace Resolution' in the pre-1970s and are unlikely
to publically recant, neither is the Soviet Union
likely to retrace its stated position. Thus, the
sole possibility still lies with the Security
Council.

Is a Cost of Collective Security The Slowing Down of Political Change?

It has been argued that "historically, the slogan
of collective security has been raised most often
by the vested interest"[33] and that collective
security produces, "un effet de dissuasion sur la
dynamique de croissance de ces systemès
politiques".[34]

Certainly, it is not so easy to distinguish
purely boundary disputes from internal questions,
as is implied by the Olaf Palme recommendations.
Mohammed Ayoob has described[35] how easy it is for
the superpowers to rival in Third World countries
given the fragility of these regimes and their
boundaries and how the regimes themselves sometimes
have to externalise their disputes to maintain
their hold. There is little question that many
internal disputes are externally aided.

One of the most vexed subjects in the long but
extremely determined attempt within the United
Nations to give a definition to the concept of
"aggression" was how much to include of the
concepts recognised as "indirect aggression" or
"economic aggressions".[36] A wide definition would
have caught more acts of aggression in its net but
would also have gone too far in preventing
inter-state economic competition. The final

definition[37]included 'indirect aggression' also
from armed force: "aggression" was, military force
who stay in a host country beyond their agreed
term, a third party state who allow their territory
to be used for acts of aggression and the sending
of armed bands or mercenaries which carry out acts
amounting to aggression. The Friendly Relations
Declaration[38] goes further in two ways, first in
enjoining against "organising, instigating
assisting or participating in acts of civil strife
or terrorist acts" likely to lead to a threat or
use of force but also second, in prohibiting, "the
use of economic, political or any other type of
measure to coerce another state"... nor "organise,
asssist, foment, finance, incite or tolerate
subversive, terrorist, or armed activities directed
towards the violent overthrow of the regime of
another state, or interfere in the civil strife in
another state."
    There is little question that if there was the
will to move towards collective security, the
conceptual battles have been fought; although such
definitions will never be perfect, they all leave
discretion to the Security Council to decide in
cases of doubt. The main point is that
international law enjoins against not only armed
force aggression but also indirect instigation of
aggression and formenting civil strife, although a
stronger view is taken of armed force. The only
exceptions are for aiding wars of liberation and in
self defence. For the first exception, fortunately,
the age of imperialism is nearly at an end so that
the United Nations will not have to engage itself
(often it is hoped) in deciding whether any act is
not an "aggression" because it aids a war of
liberation. The second area is very weak but it is
important that if the Security Council rules on the
issue, then the argument of self-defence cannot be
used. The whole point is how to ensure the Security
Council can consistently make the necessary rulings.
    Although collective security may prevent or
hinder not only attempts to bring down what from
one or other side would be regarded as
"unacceptable" regimes, it will remove one link
from the chain of causality leading to the
fragility of regimes in the Third World and allow
the internal movements to deal autonomously with
their own problems. In this sense, collective
security can be a force to strengthen democracy. It
is also a consolation that such regimes are
frequently tempted into aggression themselves as a

means of diverting attention to their human rights relations. Whatever the rights or wrongs of the Falklands war, Argentina's invasion enters this category. Such regimes may find they are on the receiving end of collective security.

A most important repercussion of effective collective security is that although brakes are put on subversion to provoke internal change, there is nothing to stop a regime inviting external assistance to halt internal change. If we are trying to establish more acceptable ground rules for what has to be agreed as a continuing global struggle of ideologies, would such invitations be in order. If the right to subvert is the counterpart to the right to ask a friendly nation to prevent internal change, then we return to international anarchy. But it is a surrender of sovereignty to deny the right of a government to ask for a friendly governemnt's help and it is not only the superpowers but some Third World Government who may object. The parallel to legalising and formalising collective security for specified states has to be elements of disarmament and this implies (at the minimum) some restraints on inviting in armed forces from friendly nations, outside of what is provided under collective security. How far such restraints can go depends on the perception at the time of governments whether they see the "knife cutting both ways"; El-Salvador government is restrained but so is Afghanistan and both are protected by collective security agreements and by implication the spheres of influence (represented within these two countries) of the superpowers are also protected. The 'restraints' formalised within a collective security agreement for a specified state will not be a surrender of ultimate sovereignty. A draft for a collective security and disarmament agreement is included for purely illustrative purposes as Annex 2.

Some recent writers[39] have advocated that indirect aggression is lawful under the principle of self-determination and equal rights (Charter Article 1), not just to end colonial régimes, but also the tyranny of an "anti-democratic" one. Two additional limiting conditions have been separately suggested first, that the U.N. is not capable of enforcing democracy and second, that the right is one of 'counter-intervention', that is if a third country helps the undemocratic regime. It is very doubtful whether it would be possible to accept the

legal references[40] as sufficient justification
for intervention, or the definitions of
"undemocratic", or the line where an insurgency
group is capable of sustaining a civil war such
that the intervention is not actually fomenting it.
All authors allow that compliance with the Charter
requires compliance with UN rulings especially
those of the Security Council. Therefore a
collective security and disarmament agreement would
not only protect a régime from such interference,
but through the accompanying disarmament there
would be the implied inhibition on inviting in
external friendly forces. For example, a collective
security agreement with Nicaragua or Afghanistan
would prohibit support for the 'CONTRAS' and the
Afghan 'rebels', and strongly inhibit third party
military support to either régime, whilst
guaranteeing the territorial integrity of the
borders of both countries. This may not be the best
short-run outturn for every party to the disputes,
but is the best long run one and is certainly the
best feasible one for the parties taken together
and the global community as a whole.

A slowing of the pace of internal change may
be a net result of collective security but it is
not a certain outcome. If so, it is still a small
price to pay for the saving of human life,
increased development, reduced forced migrations,
saving of property, decreased armaments
expenditures. It just may be that less fragile
regimes will encourage such peaceful changes in
government that they will not be, or be regarded
as, either 'revolution' or, 'counter-revolution'.

The Conditions for a Significant Reform of the Security Council

None of the permanent members of the Security
Council will be likely to take any initiatives on
the question of reform with the possible exception
of China. With the Third World acting as a block
able to defacto veto and the permanent members
individually able to veto dejure, the negative
power is rather equally distributed; the veto is
however, only a negative power. No bloc or
individual member has real positive power on the
Security Council, except that diplomacy and status
still counts; in this sense, China's position can
be crucial in a situation where the issues are
marginally poised.

But will the issues be at all poised or heavily weighted against change? There is little doubt that if such changes are going to be acceptable they will have to meet the following conditions:

1. Changes must be step by step, gradual and graduated (a kind of intra-UN confidence building exercise);

2. The superpowers will have to perceive them as maintaining an equal balance of advantage; it will be easier to help each withdraw from uncomfortable situations of potential escalation than preventing the power vacuum being filled to either superpowers disadvantage. But this must be an outcome. Collective security must not only deter or prevent aggression, it must also neutralise through "disarmament";

3. The non-aligned countries, especially the growing powers in Asia and the Pacific, would need to see the new collective security arrangements as a means of regrouping the balances of power within regional alliances, to reduce the dominance of the super-powers, whilst helping to guarantee the neutrality of the regional alliances;

4. The smaller Third World countries, moved by the global economic crisis to place a premium on marginal development over marginal defence expenditures, would be the first under the step wise progress of collective security arrangements. They would need to be satisfied that a Security Council strongly influenced by the permanent members could safeguard their sensitive security needs. Here too the past neutral role played by the Chinese on the Security Council is a major asset.

China has maintained a low profile on the Security Council, abstaining rather than vetoing,[41] using diplomacy, being brief, to the point and effective in debate.[42] After a period when China regarded peace-keeping forces as under the influence of one or other superpower, China has agreed since the end of 1981 to pay its share of expenses. China has also without any air of dominance, supported Third World and non-aligned conferences and sent non-voting delegates to ministerial meetings of the group of 77.[43] The reciprocal trust from the point of view of the Third World is not universal but is overall stronger than for any other permanent members.

A PROPOSAL TO MAKE A PERMANENT COMMISSION OF THE SECURITY COUNCIL

The Essential Tasks of a Security Council Permanent Commission

Problems within the working of the Security Council and the Secretariat support for the Security Council need to be resolved. The one feasible solution for the Security Council that may resolve the dilemma of maintaining its strong role and the unanimity rule whilst ensuring a more effective operation is to establish a subsidiary organ (under Charter article 29). The question then is what kind of subsidiary organ can undertake work for the Security Council without either duplicating or usurping the function of the Council. A second question is what links can be built with the General Assembly which satisfies the Charter, the aspirations and needs of non-permanent Security Council members and does not force the permanent members to surrender more of their perogatives than they are prepared to tolerate. The question for the Secretariat is how to strengthen it so that it is seen to be supporting the Security Council and its new organ but not in a way as to make it some kind of additional force which may undermine the Security Council. This question is of importance given the current divisions and weaknesses within the Secretariat on these issues. There is a basic question as to whether a single Secretariat body should combine the tasks of (1) peaceful settlement of disputes, (2) building up a plausible enforcement capacity and (3) parallel disarmament negotiations. Finally, technical questions arise of how to organise factfinding, conciliation, arbitration, enforcement, verification, within the Secretariat so as to be responsible to the Security Council and its new subsidiary organ. These questions will be further examined in turn.
    A peace and security Commission of the Security Council can be established under article 29 of the Charter. The object would be to have a working level body capable of acting under responsibilities and procedures agreed by the Security Council, but able to take decisions within the limits set without the veto. With this

objective, there are a number of important
questions to resolve.

How Would the Commission Differ from the Security Council Itself?

If the Commission was permanent and technical,
whilst the Council was more representative and
political, the nature of the meetings and decisions
change. Private deliberations. secret voting, and
appointment in a personal capacity would greatly
reinforce the difference. At one extreme would be a
Commission which duplicated the Security Council
but for the different voting rules and limited
mandate; at the other, would be a more bureaucratic
body. With the Security Council as the political
master, it would be possible to seek for a more
independent minded Commission constituted to take
strong decisions, as far as possible by concensus.
      Apart from ensuring members of the Commission
were nominated in such a way as to ensure the Third
World and non-aligned were sufficiently
represented, there would need to be some formal
links to the General Assembly. The existence of an
effective Commission of the Council would alter the
attitudes within the General Assembly Committees.
Clearly the main committees (First Committee, Sixth
Committee and Special Political Affairs) are too
large, formal, and temporary, to be the close
watchdog on behalf of the General Assembly. The
Charter Committee is a body mainly devoted to legal
questions; however either the Special Committee on
peace-keeping could cover the requirements; or the
proposed Ad-Hoc Committee on Internationa' Peace
and Security, apprehension of which by the Security
Council would fade once the Commission became
active. The advent of the Commission should allow
some rationalisation of the security related
committee structure in the General Assembly.[44]
The Uniting For Peace Resolution would also become
an anachronism if the Commission was effective. The
amalgamated Ad-Hoc and Special Peacekeeping
Committee (abbreviated to Ad-Hoc Committee) could
be permanent, with open debates and open voting.
The officers could meet with, and even be invited
to meetings of the Commission at the discretion of
the Commission, and the meetings could be on the
same subjects as the Commission and at the same
time. This would make the General Assembly Ad-hoc
Committee a quite powerful watchdog and advisory
force. The Security Council would continue to

report to the General Assembly and so would the
Ad-hoc Committee.

How Would Commissioners be Chosen?

Although the simplest way of achieving an
acceptable balance of forces is to have the members
of the Security Council nominate Commissioners, it
will give the permanent members longer serving
Commissioners than other Council members. The
Commissioners need not be nationals of the country
appointing but are likely to be in most cases and
it would seem pointless and unfair to depose a
really effective Commissioner from a Third World
non-aligned country just because the two year term
of his senior was over. It would be better that the
permanent members would appoint their own
Commissioners and the others would be appointed by
meetings of the regional non-aligned groupings.
Whenever a Commissioner had to be changed, it might
be useful to establish a custom for the country on
the Security Council to nominate its own national
if a suitable candidate was available.
Commissioners could serve for an unlimited period
and could elect their Chairmen who also would not
have any time limit set. Commissioners could be
asked to resign by the Chairman, by the President
of the Security Council in the first instance, with
a final appeal on a procedural vote of the whole
Security Council.

How Would Commissioners Function in Relation to the Secretariat?

It would probably work more effectively if
Commissioners could be made responsible for one or
more problem areas. Each problem area could have a
small secretariat staff and specialist groups of
the Secretariat could service these problem areas
as priority tasks. The Secretariat would be
responsble to the Commissioners, the Commission as
a whole and the Secretary-General, and as with the
servicing of such bodies as the Joint Inspection
Unit, there is unlikely to be much stress as a
result of dual responsibilities, especially if the
Commission as a whole was allocated a clearly
defined departmental regrouping. All the budgeted
time of the allocated department would be to the
work of the Commission and nowhere else: the
Commissioners would be wholly responsible for
reports under their name and the Secretariat would

be there to assist them. A lot of the work of
existing departments would be taken over including
the offices of the Special Representatives for
Namibia and Afghanistan which would signify a
return to the Security Council of functions which
by force of circumstances had to be undertaken
closely under the Secretary-General, greatly
overloading his personal responsibilities and
political exposure.

THE RANGE OF ACTIVITIES OF THE COMMISSION

The range of activities controlled by the
Commission should determine the organisation of the
Secretariat services which would support the
Commission. Six major areas can be identified:

1.   Information gathering;
2.   Peaceful settlement of disputes;
3.   Economic santions;
4.   Support for regional collective agreements;
5.   Military enforcement/peace-keeping procedures;
6.   Parallel disarmament negotiations.

Information Gathering

Three suggestions require exploration: (i) using a
network of UN offices to improve the two way flow
of information, (ii) increasing and systematising
fact finding missions, (iii) setting up an
independent UN sattelite monitoring.

UN Network of Offices. The Commission will require
up to date and accurate information on problems
separate from the partial reports given by parties
to a dispute. This information could come from a
quasi-diplomatic service, fact-finding missions and
some form of independent sattelite monitoring. All
of these have been discussed and reviewed
before.[45] As regards the quasi-diplomatic
service, there is certainly no need to look farther
than the existing offices of the UNDP Resident
Representative who is already looked upon as the
Ambassador of the UN in the country concerned and
in many countries now is the "Coordinator" of the
UN System within the country, having powers over
even the semi-independent UN System agencies. The
RRUNDP makes himself familiar with the political
problems in the country and is a confidant of
government officials and other members of the

114

diplomatic corps. The average standard of officer acting as a Resident Representative is high and justifies the extra trust and responsibility. The Secretary General would agree with his colleagues in the agencies a person to represent the System (if necessary for a group of countries) in each of the major capitals where the System was represented but there was no UN office or RRUNDP (most developed countries have RRUNDP).

Fact-finding Missions. UN fact finding missions are a regular part of UN Secretariat life; they can be made up of members of the Secretariat or from a high level consultant roster. Most countries would accept them. Where a problem was particularly complex the RRUNDP would welcome an independent assessment which could be made available to the parties in dispute and be more hard-hitting, whereas the RRUNDP's reports would need to be private to the Secretary-General.

Independent Monitoring. Satellite monitoring is the principal source of information open for an independent UN System of monitoring of international crises. The group of experts reporting on the feasibility of a UN agency to verify disarmament agreements and monitoring international crises concluded on the ideas technical and legal feasibility.[46]

> "The group of experts reached the conclusion that monitoring by satellite of international crises situations is technically feasible and that ISMA could make an effective contribution in the observation from space of military aspects related to the inception and development of conflict. The type of monitoring envisaged would include verification of compliance with cease-fire arrangements; surveillance of demilitarised zones; provision of evidence of border violations or preparations for aggression; and any other mission which states or the United Nations may assign to the agency that would be consistent with its constitution."

The experts advised placing the recommended new agency under the General Assembly; it rejected the Security Council despite the fact that "the chances for participation of the Space Powers in the Agency's work would be improved" because this advantage would be counterbalanced by the need to obtain the unanimous vote of the permanent members for decisions. If the Agency was placed under the recommended Commission, then this obstacle would be removed. There has been no substantive progress in ISMA since the report in 1983, although the idea is certainly not dead. The principal objections from the superpowers that they would pay a large part of the costs when they already have the information may be outweighed by the willingness to accept third party verification of superpower agreements. The advent of anti-satellite weapons may make a somewhat more inviolated communication system an attractive step to the superpowers. The objection from many non-super power countries that their security information will be generally known still outweighs the fact that the superpowers already have it; but there were ways suggested in the 1983 report of reserving the information for the parties to the dispute.

Peaceful Settlement of Disputes

Nigeria, Philippines and Romania came in 1983 to the Special Committees of the General Assembly in the Charter[47] with a proposal to set up a good office commission. It was criticised because it was not wholly a creature of either the Security Council or the General Assembly, and had powers of automatic reference and universal membership; without any backing from a more powerful Security Council mandate the proposal would have insufficient status. In the same way, despite the status of his position, good office missions by the Secretary-General lack the power of either funding or enforcement of a superpower; the extra objectivity of a UN Secretary-General is an asset, but is not sufficient in itself.[48]

Finally, because there has been no likelihood of improving the keeping of agreements, there has been no progress on UN initiatives to strengthen disputes settlement procedures. Recent attempts to set up a Commission independent from the General Assembly or the Security Council were criticised on grounds of size, duplicating existing procedures, and the automatic procedure which clashed with the principle of the free choice of means (for the solution of disputes). The recommended Commission, acting with the full authority of the Security Council, has the Charter powers (articles 33-38) to call the parties together and make recommendations.

It can also ask the ICJ for an advisory opinion as
well as appoint an arbitrator. The Commission
would need to have agreed conciliation, and
arbitration procedures related to advice from the
ICJ and linked to its peace-keeping and enforcement
powers. Some thought would need to be given to how
this procedure would work in practice. One point is
certain, the enforcement powers are an essential
backstopping to any attempt to inaugurate agreed
peaceful dispute settlement procedures.

The proposed Commissioner himself could act as
mediator in disputes, supported by his Secretariat.
If mediation failed, then it is suggested there
would be automatic reference to arbitration with,
where regarded as helpful by any party to the
disputes, an advisory opinion on the law involved
requested from the ICJ. The arbitration report
would be initially drawn up by the Commissioner and
finally decided upon by the whole Commission.

Parties to an arbitration should be able to
appeal to the Security Council and/or the ICJ but
where parties chose the Security Council and the
Council accepted the request to deal with the
questions, then the decision would be final. Figure
5.1 represents the recommended process. The object
of the process is to ensure that over time as many
as possible of the appeals to the Security Council
would be rejected as not receivable and the grounds
for this would be slowly built up beginning with
guidelines set by the Security Council and then
case precedents and then renewed guidelines.

The Security Council on its procedural vote
(Step 6) could 'claw back' any issue or case based
on 'exigencies', but it should become increasingly
unacceptable to do this if guidelines and
precedents are clear. If a 'claw back' decision
under step (6) was itself a substantive rather than
as recommended here, a procedural vote, then the
likelihood of a veto deciding or not deciding the
issue (i.e., leaving it in the air) is not greatly
reduced by the whole process above; the prior work
of the Security Council Commissioner, Secretariat
and Commission, would count for very little in
these cases.

Only if the Security Council rejects an appeal
as not receivable would a party to a dispute be
able to appeal to the ICJ which would prevent the
status of the Council being impaired.

The above process for the most part accepts
the principle of the 'free choice of means'; the

Figure 5.1

Peaceful Settlement of Disputes Process

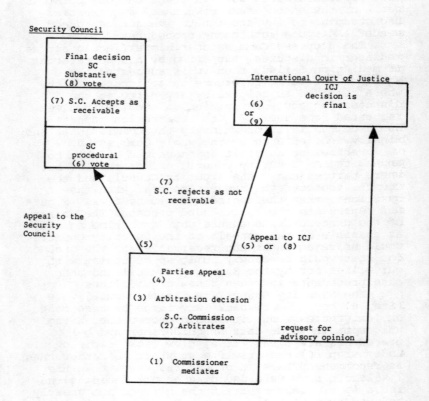

automatic arbitration process would apply only if the parties did not choose another arbitration forum whose decisions they agreed to accept. The parties also have the choice to appeal either to the Security Council or the ICJ.

Because the ICJ, even if it was strengthened to cater for more and more rapid decisions, would still take considerable time, parties should not be able to use it as a delaying tactic whilst they started or continued to use aggression. The Security Council Commission would commence peace-keeping or enforcement procedures if either party used force, notwithstanding an appeal to the ICJ.

Economic Sanctions

There is such a need for some type of sanction below the level of "enforcement", under Article 42 of the Charter, that economic sanctions have had a persistence and are likely to continue to do so, despite the considerable criticism against them that has evolved.[49] There are certain lessons from the experiences of international economic sanctions:[50]

1. International economic sanctions are more powerful than individual national sanctions and they should not be confused together;
2. a considerable effort is needed to obtain widespread agreement for the operation of sanctions because so many public and private sector agencies are involved;
3. Some of the reluctance to see sanctions work arises from the fear of member states that a time may come when sanctions are applied to them;
4. the cost of sanctions can be unfairly high on neighbouring small states and so far aid has not counterbalanced;
5. Sanction processes have to be swifter than the slow progress from, 'selective optional' through 'selective mandatory' to 'comprehensive mandatory' sanctions;
6. A central coordinating unit with independent sources of information and strong links to key national areas of control is essential. So much the better if it would be possible to operate (perhaps through INTERPOL) an independent right of search;
7. Sanctions have to be particularised and well

researched to the target states special
vulnerabilities; exports are easier to reduce
in general; the impact of sanctions on imports
is often more on cost or prices than total
supply and the general market situation at the
time is therefore important.

Unless there is some particular vulnerable area
(such as oil) where a tight embargo may be imposed,
the effects are bound to be slow acting. However,
once a government refuses an arbitration decision
it is not only sanctions which may be authorised
but subversion is legitimised. For 'subversion',
either considerable finance needs to be available
or commercial, financial and multinational industry
interests have to be 'on the side of' the United
Nations action or able to be mobilised once the
decisions are taken. Although the IMF/World Bank
group are to ignore ideologies in their policies
towards their members, so of course does the United
Nations as a whole. The Bank Group do not have to
'obey' Security Council decisions but only to give
due regard to these decisions; this may be
sufficient.

A dilemma with non-military sanctions is that
the number of agencies, sectors and countries
involved may be relatively large. Military
sanctions although more serious are relatively
self-contained. For the initial effort at
collective security for the Third World, the
machinery required for effective economic sanctions
may be top heavy.

Because economic sanctions are a relatively
high profile activity (requiring broad, if not
universal government/private sector consent), for
the initial problems of the Commission, the aim
should be highly selective well aimed activities
involving more positive attempts at subversion or
coercion than just sanctions and combined with
enforcement i.e., naval blockade. It may be
paradoxical that only after the Commission has
established itself and is fully accepted, that
economic sanctions can be a more articulated and
positive peace-keeping weapon in the armoury of the
Security Council.

The ground rules circumscribing the promotion
of legalised subversion will need to be carefully
layed down as the United Nations must not be
associated with distasteful, inhuman or corrupting
activities. In preference to supporting subversion
where the result is self contaminating, the

Commission should be advised to recommend economic
sanctions or finally, enforcement.

A permanent sanctions secretariat should be
attributed to the Commission which is relatively
small and can bring together on an _ad-hoc_ basis
sub-commissions required to deal with specific
problems. The location within the Commission allows
the maximum coordination between the military
forces made available for enforcement and the
economic sanctions secretariat. The funds made
available for economic sanctions can be budgeted
along with those for peace-keeping and enforcement
to deal with each problem allocated to particular
Commissioners. The cost of economic sanctions for
the UN as an organisation would rise considerably
if compensatory payments are required for the
innocent countries who are caught in the squeeze.
These could be high and difficult to fund. Long
term, some compensatory arrangements could be
considered, but initially, while the Commission
gains broad status, it would greatly assist the
argument for collective security if compensation
was not included as costs to be shared on the basis
of the proportionate assessment.

Strengthening of Regional Pacts of Collective Security

Regional collective security was seen by the
charter as an alternative to UN direct enforcement.
Not much has been done by the UN to strengthen
regional collective security capacity because
regional arrangements have gained their strength
from their own partiality, to which the UN cannot
be party.

Where regional collective security pacts were
willing to enter into a covenant not to use
collective regional security against non-members
without the agreement of the Security Council or
its Commission, then this pact could be technically
and militarily supported. As long as a regional
action dealt only with members and there was no
appeal to the Commission to arbitrate then the UN
is not involved.

UN troops which were pledged to help
strengthen a regional collective security pact must
always be used in the name of the UN itself, to
enforce peace even within the countries of the pact
and for that to happen, the Commission would have
needed to arbitrate accordingly. For a collective
security pact to use force legitimately on

Collective Security and Disarmament

countries outside the pact, the concurrence of the
Security Council is also necessary. The Commission
would then have a role to strengthen such pacts as
were prepared to covenant with the UN.

Peace-keeping and Enforcement

The flexibility that enforcement could give would
cause problems for UN force commanders without
clear guidelines, but it will be appreciated that
the capacity to use enforcement in general does not
mean it has to be used. It has been found for
peace-keeping forces that for tactical, diplomatic
and even military reasons (fewer troops necessary),
troops who interpose and shoot, if at all, only in
the strictest definition of self-defence, are more
successful than larger forces who try and shoot
out. If that is so, then for the same reasons, the
same tactics will apply. Also where impartiality is
essential, agreement to intervene to preserve peace
can be sought from all parties with the object of
maximising the consent of the parties to actions
taken.

If one party in the arbitration uses force to
prevent the decision in the arbitration being
carried out, then it is likely that permission to
intervene will be impossible to obtain. In many
cases as the Palme Commission appreciated, it may
be just necessary to station troops in the
aggrieved party's country with that party's full
approval. The number of cases where enforcement has
to take place in a country which refuses permission
will ultimately be small. Here the need to be
impartial is lessened. One of the difficulties with
the multinational forces in Lebanon was that they
needed to be impartial in a role which required
impartiality and were not. If troops are stationed
in the country of an aggressor the restraints of
impartiality are removed.

One of the major problems about enforcement is
the fear of being dragged stage by stage into a
total war commitment (even if only conventional
war) against an aggressor in the name of the UN. To
some degree, greater commitment by member countries
to supply troops or permanent standby forces would
reduce this worry, but it will not be wholly
removed without some limits being set. Such limits
are also not easy to set without encouraging an
aggressor to aim to surpass them. A long drawn out,
costly, brutal enforcement action could rebound on
the name of the UN and all it stands for. There is

no institutional trick which can remove this fear although clear related military and political objectives and the knowledge that the UN does not go to war except as a last resort, that it will not go to war over any ideology, religion or against any people, should help ameliorate it. In addition, the military limits should be set initially high to act not only as a major deterrent but also to achieve the military objects quickly. Finally, as was written under economic sanctions, the knowledge and increasing possibilities of non-military subversion and sanctions is such that the clear military option will be decreasingly less necessary. The number of occurrences that a government will risk an act of aggression or illegal subversion will grow smaller if collective security becomes effective; initially though the cases will be greater.

One of the initially unlooked for impacts of collective security success will be that the UN will have to be prepared to become involved in supervising internal elections as a government is likely to fall in a regime that loses an enforcement contest with the UN. The experience from Rhodesia and the preparations that have been made for Namibia can also be brought together in the Commission Secretariat.

Disarmament

The disarmament associated with Third World Collective Security can only be a small proportion of the total question of disarmament but in the direct trade off against development and in direct prevention of human suffering the benefits are disproportionately large.

The expert group report[51] encouraged "Parallelism and Coordination of measures in both its disarmament and the security fields...". From the international collective security side, the above measures should provide the basis for the first moves. Disarmament can be suggested in discrete stages whilst commitment to collective security should be open ended. It would appear that the form which would best guarantee collective security would be a contractual agreement with each country entered into with the Security Council of the United Nations. These collective security agreements could run in parallel with specific military forces agreements under article 43 of the UN Charter, some of which would be for all collective security agreements and some may cover named countries.

The terms of a collective security/disarmament agreement would be very specific, depending upon the relevant agreements under Article 43, and the problems of timing and physical difficulty of delivering armed forces to particular locations. The more 'cast-iron' the security agreement proposed, the more demanding could be the terms of the staged process of disarmament. The Annex 2 is an attempt to illustrate what a collective security and disarmament agreement might look like, highlighting some of the conceptual, legal, financial and logistical problems that will require solution.

An essential part of any disarmament and collective security agreement is that a country who signed is 'enjoined' not to invite in forces from friendly government to put down internal opposition, whilst still retaining the sovereign right to do so. Governments will always insist on retaining para-military forces for internal use and agreements will have to allow wide flexibility on their extent. Governments will then be faced with the choice of increased security against external aggression ('direct' and 'indirect') and reduced external protection against internal opposition. If countries either choose not to sign so as to retain the right to invite external forces to restrain internal opposition or exert their ultimate sovereignty and do so within the agreement, then it will be clearer, than it is now, that a system of sovereign nation states cooperating in a United Nations cannot function. The test can only be made once an effective collective security and disarmament procedure is put in place.

As each country or block of countries agrees or requests a collective security/disarmament agreement, the work of the Commission will slowly grow. It does not have to grow too fast and in fact if it did so, the Commission may be faced with too many problems too quickly.

If the Commission felt able to tackle a major problem, it could invite the parties or blocs of countries pertaining to the problem to sign collective security/disarmament agreements.

Countries would, it is hoped, sign willingly. The Commission would act against an aggressor whether it was party to the agreement or not. If the aggressor state had explicitly refused the terms of such an agreement, it could not any longer claim its actions were justified by self defence under the Charter, Article 51.

For the main part, the Commission would confine itself to arbitrating where at least one member state was party to a collective security/disarmament agreement. An appeal to the Security Council by a non-signatory state against an arbitration decision would be less likely to be receiveable. Nothing precludes either the Commission or the Security Council from taking up a problem under Chapters Vl and Vll of the Charter but there is no obligation to be involved, unless the requesting State has a signed agreement. This will take the pressure off the Security Council Commission and allow it to build up its strength on solid foundations of precedent and broad concensus.

COSTING OF THE COMMISSION

How much will it cost and who will pay are two inevitable questions.

The cost

Currently, the UN is spending about US$260 million per annum on peace and security. The estimate of US$519 million for the budget biennium 1984 and 1985 is broken down in table 1. Approximately 90% of the biennium figure, i.e., US$470 million goes on peace-keeping forces of which UNIFIL (S. Lebanon) takes US$360 million. The amount shown for the peace-keeping forces is an underestimate as the countries contributing pay their own forces salaries and some other costs (of the 6 monthly total US$51 million for UNFICYP (Cyprus), the countries contributing forces pay US$36.3 million or 71%. Roughly, the annual overheads of peace and security administration of US$50 million represents 10% of the total UN peace and security effort, including country contributions, of US$500 million.

The advent of the new Security Council Commission could bring about some savings from the above costs. The diversion of say, $10 million from the total of US$50 million overheads is the upper limit of possibility but the real question mark applies to Lebanon and Cyprus. An arbitration decision could be the basis of solid agreements in Cyprus, but combined enforcement and peace-keeping would be necessary to keep the factions apart in Lebanon long enough to allow UN troop withdrawal.

Also, without a Middle East settlement, the
situation would always threaten to erupt. The
Commission could not start off with the most
explosive issues unless its mandate was understood
to be remedial and therefore long drawn out and
expensive. The costs of UNIFIL in Lebanon must, for
these calculations, be assumed to continue.
      The costs of peace-keeping by the Security
Council Commission could grow if overall, its work
was a success. This would imply that countries were
disarming and relying on the Commission for dispute
settlement, that is, that UN collective security
was substituting for national arms expenditures.
Third World armament expenditures currently amount
to close to US$115 billion per annum; only a small
reduction is necessary to pay for the extra costs
of UN peace and security measures for the Third
World. The costs that should be studied are the
costs incurred at an early stage of the work of the
Commission prior to major disarmament agreements,
i.e. the 'worst' case scenario. This occurs where
costs may be low but the method of cost recovery
has not been well established. Table 5.2 presents
an estimate of costs detailed item by item in annex
1. The overall costs at 1985 prices (say, by the
5th year of operation) are thus estimated to be
US$500 million p.a. plus the additional $350
million p.a. minus cost savings of about $40
million (UNFICYP costs plus some overheads). These
costs of US$800 million need to be set alongside
the savings anticipated from reduction in the
US$115 billion per annum currently spent by the
Third World on armaments plus extra benefits from
disasters avoided. The additional net costs of
US$310 million will also increase the overall
effectiveness of a significant portion of the
existing UN and Peace and Security expenditures of
US$500 million.

Funding

Ultimately, it makes sense that those countries
that benefit from disarmament and collective
security agreements should pay a portion of the
costs but initially the global community should
share the costs as an investment in world peace in
which all would gain.
      There are a number of formulae and if the
debate continues to that stage of detail all of
them should be examined. One suggestion is that
countries should pay a proportion of the ratio of

Table 5.1 Budget and Staff of the United Nations Organs Concerned with Peace and Security for Biennium 1984/85

	Budget Biennial 1984/85 (US$000's)	Professional staff	Total Staff
		(numbers)	
Secretary General and Office	6,866	25	62
Special Political Affairs	3,232	15	29
Special Polical Questions	2,667	4	7
Field Operations	2,600	14	31
Security Council and Office	10,890	58	94
Special Missions (Peacekeeping)	54,462	8	594
Disarmament	8,893	31	57
Namibia	9,949	14	33
Estimated (direct) total	99,559	169	872
*plus 20% of General Assembly	878	2	4
Estimated total	100,437	171	876
plus**UNIFIL	360,000		
**UNFICYP	59,000		
	519,000		

* Estimated time spent by General Assembly and the Committees on peace and security issues.

**Excludes country payment for own forces.
Source: Future A/38/6 Section 2A and Official Document Security Council.

Table 5.2   Rough Costing of the Security Council
Peace and Security Commission

		Per annum costs US$000's
1.	Commission	
	1.1 Commissioners	2,500
	1.2 Staff	3,750
2.	Factfinding	
	2.1 Strengthening RRUNDP's	4,500
	2.2 Consultant missions	200
	2.3 ISMA (Phase I)	32,000
3.	Observer forces	7,000
4.	Peace keeping forces (additional to current costs)	140,000
5.	Economic Sanctions	28,000
6.	Enforcement (additional to peace-keeping)	91,000
7.	Contribution to Standby Forces	
	7.1 Troops on standby	12,000
	7.2 Amortisation and maintenance stockpile	30,000
	Total	350,950

defence to total government expenditure at the time[52] of their signing an agreement, but that there is a grace period in which they do not pay. This period should be a maximum of ten years for countries signing in the first year and declining successively by one year thereafter giving an incentive to early signing. Otherwise, costs are loaded on to the normal UN contribution formula. By the eleventh year all direct UN costs (other than the work of the Security Council, the Commission and the Secretariat) should be covered by a special collective security contribution.

The above formula creates an investment period in which all pay and a running cost where those who benefit most pay most. It makes it an article of faith that there will be collective security gains for the Third World and that the benefits in reduced national defence expenditures will be sufficient that paying for collective security is a relatively small burden. For the developed countries, their share will be amply justified by the lower risks of their alliances being pulled into escalating confrontations, by the greater isolation of terrorist activities and lower risks of nuclear proliferation.

SUMMARY

Are we ignoring forty years of history in proposing a change in the procedures of the Security Council. That history has been examined and comfirmed the futility of such recommendations; the adoption by the General Assembly of responsibilities in peace and security unlooked for by the Charter authors has been an illustration of the desperate attempts to escape from the Security Council impasse. What has changed to justify renewed effort?

The call by the Secretary-General for changed methods and attitudes in the Security Council is a manifestation that there is no other viable pathway. Economic and social reforms will take too long; the General Assembly is inhibited by the Charter and not accepted by the permanent members of the Security Council as the valid forum – the unweighted voting of the General Assembly cannot be a sufficient authority to resolve the most fundamental power relationship problems facing countries, not least the countries of the Third World. Regional collective security pacts are either too partial, and only confirm the intrusion of superpower politics into more local problems, or

129

are so divided that they cannot act decisively,
especially as the Charter enforcement powers under
Chapter VII have not supported them. Even detente
between the superpowers has been tried and has
neither resulted in agreement on how to improve
collective security nor how to reform and use the
Security Council more effectively; the immediate
past has seen the very reverse of detente and an
intensification of superpower rivalry especially
for influence amongst the Third World and
non-aligned.

In the past, suggested reforms of the Security
Council have been too drastic; the ideas put
forward here do not abolish or amend the veto; they
simply and gradually weight it down a little; the
weights only grow heavier as concensus and
precedent build up in the subsidiary organ of the
Security Council Commission. More important there
is greater appreciation of the growing powers and
prestige of the Third World as a bloc (certainly as
it operates in the Security Council and General
Assembly) and particular Third World and
non-aligned countries. There is also real worry
about the extent of terrorist activities arising
from conflicts within the Third World and how
nuclear proliferation and terrorism may become
interrelated. Changing defence strategies are of
themselves causing some significant reassessment of
the position by both superpowers and European and
Eastern Asia and the Pacific region countries.
Superpower hegomony and 'Mutually Assured
Destruction' no longer are the restraining forces
that they were over the previous 40 years and the
restraints are perceived as growing less as time
passes.

Disarmament is inextricably linked to
collective security not simply because national
armaments would be less necessary, but also because
it is the only solution to prevent a permanent
ossification of internal politics. Within the
context of a continued collective
security/disarmament agreement,countries may be
willing to forego their right to invite armed
assistance from a friendly power. If a regime
facing internal opposition and growing weaker was
able to bolster its strength by calling on friendly
regimes, the course of internal political change
(in whatever direction) could be greatly inhibited.
Currently, the threat of external direct and
indirect aggression is some counterweight to this
use of friendly regimes and collective security

would reduce that counterweight. Giving explicit recognition to this unpalatable conclusion may help to bring the discussion about collective security and disarmament closer to the practical level where real dialogue can occur.

From a practical point of view, collective security and (conventional) disarmament should be promoted together. The focus is a collective security and disarmament agreement. Parallel with the Secretariat work to establish these agreements is the machinery of fact-finding, mediation, arbitration, enforcement and disarmament. The Commission of the Security Council would regulate its work by giving absolute priority to problems referred by a signatory country to which there was a UN obligation and whose defence against any direct aggression would not wait for any prior legal stages of the agreed process. Outside the area of these agreements, the Commission could allow problems to wash over it, choosing those which it could handle at an early stage, until it was well founded and strong enough to deal with more complex areas. The number of agreements and the means to honour them would grow in parallel.

If there is not the most widespread support and cooperation for economic sanctions, the task of applying them can be likened to holding back flowing water with a sieve. Many departments of many governments must cooperate to make sanctions effective, supported by a powerful and accepted UN control and coordinating group. The top heavy nature of the machinery at the early stages of the work of the Security Council Commission is only partly offset by the more acceptable nature of economic as against military force sanctions. The possibility of legalising subversion through the increasingly related UN System monetary and development finance institution's linked to the state and private finance markets is as yet an unexplored option.

The annual cost of existing and anticipated UN activities related to the responsibilities of the recommended Security Council Peace and Security Commission would be US$800 million which is 0.7% of the estimated annual expenditure by the Third World on defence. On any reasonable assumption a ten year investment by the global community must be worthwhile; if then direct costs are defrayed by a contribution by the agreement signatory countries, there would only have to be disarmament by less than 0.7% for costs to be covered. Despite continued reliance by countries on their national military forces, even after collective security is put in place, our sights for disarmament can be set higher than that.

Notes to Chapter 5.

1. Maurice Bertrand – "Contribution à une reflexion sur la réform des Nations Unies", UN Corp common d'Inspection, Genève, 1985 (JIU/REP/85/9).,

2. James O.C. Jonah "Disarmament and the Strenthening of United Nations Machinery to Maintain International Peace and Security", Disarmament, UN Vol. VII; No. 3, Autumn 1984, p.96.

3. Mohammed Ayoob – "International Affairs Vol: 60: No. 1 Winter 1984.

4. GA/36/356(E.82.IX.1), Table III.5.

5. A. Kemp – "The Third World Impact of Super Power Military Competition: Current Research on Peace and Violence", Vol. VII No. 2–3 1984.

6. Ibid, Mohammed Ayoob; listed as (1) test new weapons; (2) arms sales; (3) recycle petrodollars; (4) pay for their R and D; (5) test limits of adversary persistence; (6) impress allies; (7) maintain access to raw materials.

7. A. Beker – "Disarmament without Order", Greenwood Press, 1985.

8. The Group has still only a negative power to vote down a resolution; its positive role is countered by the permanent members potential veto.

9. GA/36/597, pp 46–47; the general principles of coordination of security and disarmament measures were established.

10. Independent Commission on Disarmament and Security Issues – "Common Security: A Programme for Disarmament" Pan Books, London, 1982 pp 126–134, pp 162–167.

11. A/S–12/32, pp 44–46.

12. Ibid. Mohammed Ayoob, International Affairs, Winter 1984 explains the forces which cause the difficulty in separating internal and external security issues.

13. R. L. Jackson – "The Non-aligned, the UN and the Superpowers" Council on Foreign Relations, Praeger 1983.

14. B. Urquhart – "International Peace and Security", Foreign Affairs Vol. 60, No.1, Fall 1981, p.14.
15. Reporting of Practice of United Nations Organs, Supplement No. 4, Vol. 1, Articles 1–54 of the Charter p. 124.
16. ICJ advisory opinion, "Certain Expenses of UN" (20 VII 62) p.172.
17. The USSR questioned this in its submission to the ICJ and elsewhere. See the dissenting opinion of Judge Koretsky in 20 VII 62, pp 259–260.
18. For example Security Council Resolution of 31st October 1956.
19. V.F. Petrovsky – "The Soviet Concept of Security", UNIDIR 1985. Sales No. GV/E. 85 0.2 p.32.
20. Ibid. Jackson p.116.
21. E. McWhinney – "United Nations Law Making", Holmes and Meier/UNESCO Press, 1984, p.151.
22. Report of the Secretary–General on the Work of the Organisation September 1982 GA.37/1.
23. Note by the President of the Security Council S15971 12 September 1983 and Report of the Security Council to the General Assembly, GA.39/2.
24. GA/38/271 and S/15830.
25. GA/37/100 E, 38/73 H, 39/63K.
26. GA/37/119, 38/191 and 39/158.
27. GA/38/141, 39/88.
28. Mr Gbeho of Ghana. A/C.1/39/PV.59, pp 118–120
29. GA38/191.
30. Report GA/39/33.
31. Apart from the guidelines in S/11052/Rev.1. 27 October 1973.
32. Mr G.L. Sherry at the 31st Pugwash Conference expressed this point of view succinctly; see Proceedings Report (Banff 1981) p.269. "There are those who have argued that if we would only organise the United Nations a bit differently, if we tinkered with its debating and voting procedures (and made sure that rules of procedure were observed), if we codified methods of peaceful settlement, broadened the functions of the Secretary–General and set up a permanent peace-keeping force, the United Nations would become significantly more effective. In fact, while improvements under some of these headings would obviously be valuable and are in some cases overdue, the resulting benefits

would be marginal. The existing ponderous machinery can work very well and perform wonders when there is the political consensus and will to give it momentum. Without that consensus and will the best procedures would be in vain."

33. M.V. Naidu - "Collective Security and the United Nations" New York, 1974.

34. K.Gaule - "Cooperation entre les Etats Africains en Matiers de Dèfense" Nigerian Institute of International Affairs July 1981, Lagos, Nigeria (Mimeo).

35. Ibid. Mohammed Ayoob, International Affairs, Winter 1984.

36. Defined in document A/2211 Report by the Secretary-General to 7th General Assembly, 1952.

37. For a review of the history to define "aggression" in international law,see B.B. Ferencz- "Defining International Aggression: The Search for World Peace", Oceana publications. Vol.2. 1975. The UN General Assembly Resolution which agreed the definition is GA 3314 (XXIX).

38. "The (1970) Declaration of Principles of International Law concerning the Friendly Relations and Cooperation Among States in accordance with the Charter of the United Nations", Resolution 2625(XXV).

39. (i) M. Reisman - "Coercion and Self-determination: constraining Charter Article 2(4)", American Journal of International Law, Vol. 78 No 3, 1984. (ii) L. N. Cutler - "The Right to Intervene", Foreign Affairs, Fall 1985.

40. Charter Article 1 and International covenant on Civil and Political Rights, 1966, Article 1.

41. Between 1971 and 1976 China used the veto twice in 37 votes (the second time jointly) and since then (up to 1980) not at all.

42. S.S. Kim - "China, the United Nations and World Order", Princeton University Press, 1979.

43. S.S. Kim (Editor) - "China and the Third World", Westview Press, 1984.

44. Special Political Affairs could amalgamate with the First Committee and the Sixth Committee would cease to have matters pushed to it beyond its legal scope.

45. See Ibid Shelly p. 277.

46. UN – "The Implications of Establishing an International Satellite Monitoring Agency", New York 1983, E.83.IX.3. pp. 67.
47. GA 38/343; also GA/39/33.
48. Secretary-General's have been wary of using their 'good office' functions where they were likely to fail; even Dag Hammarskjold was very selective and wished to be invited by the concerned parties before he would intervene. B. Urquhart – "Hammarskjold" Harper 1972, p.309.
49. The "puzzling" continued use of sanctions despite the critiques is examined by J. Maynall –" The Sanctions Problem in International Economic Relations: reflections in the light of experience", International Affairs. Vol: 60. No. 4. Autumn 1984. A list of criticisms can be exhaustively read in M.S. Daoudi and M.S. Dajani – "Economic Sanctions: Ideals and Experience", Routledge and Kegan Paul London, 1983, appendix 2.
50. League of Nations: Yugoslavia 1921, Paraguay 1934, Italy 1935-6; United Nations: Spain 1946, China 1951, N. Korea 1951, South Africa 1963, Rhodesia Nov. 1965-Dec 1979.
51. Ibid. A/36/597 (E.821X.4), p.9.
52. An average of the five previous years.

Chapter Six

CONCLUSION

EXISTING BALANCES OF POWER

Despite the dissatisfaction with the voting systems
in the General Assembly and Economic and Social
Council by the industrialised countries, the
existing, albeit very precarious, balances must
either be preserved or replaced deliberately with
more efficient structures having an equal balance
of power and a chance of longevity. Figure 6.1
shows the North/South and East/West existing
balance of power in the UN System. The main balance
is between North and South but probably the most
striking point is that the East can only balance
the west by maintaining a weak System and
exploiting the North/South divisions. The
North/West quadrant of figure 6.1 suggests much
greater control over the UN System than the
North/East quadrant.
     The developed countries have more
representatives present and attending committees of
the General Assembly and they are more active in
the important committees like the Fifth (Financial)
Committee. The tradition of always having the
permanent members on any committee also strengthens
their hand. Contact men from regional blocks come
from the most important developing countries; the
mini-states do not have much impact on decision
making. In the specialised agency governing bodies
the developed countries are also more heavily
represented than their weighting in the main
assemblies.
     In all the specialised agencies, voluntary
funds are controlled by the industrialised
countries and votes in the executive bodies of
these agencies are much more weighted to the
industrialised countries than in the assemblies.

Figure 6.1 Existing Balance of Power in the UN

N

Financial Power (i.e., 5th Committee);
Governing Bodies of most Organs;
Strong and active representation;
Veto Power Permanent members and seats on
all main committees of System;

Weak competitive agencies
and
Secretariat

W

IMF/World Bank Group/GATT;
voluntary funding UNDP and
all programmes of System
outside regular budget;

E

General Assembly
and
Economic and Social Council
Voting power;
Negative blocking power in Security Council;
Control of All assemblies of System agencies;

S

137

Conclusion

The assemblies can pass resolutions and make
general policy statements but the executive bodies
control the real spending and the programmes.
   For the Security Council, the support to the
developing countries given by China and Russia as
well as the strength of the combined developing
country block vote also counter balances the veto
power of the 'Western' developed countries,
although it does not lead to positive decisions.
   Any new alignment has to provide a much
greater influence of the North/East to give it a
stake in a stronger and more efficient UN System.
Any change in the voting structure of the General
Assembly which puts decisive power in the hands of
the North and West industrialised countries and
diminishes the current control by the non-aligned
South, would be totally unacceptable to the
socialist North and East. It would return us to the
equally dark days immediately after the Second
World War when the USSR did not contribute to any
enhancement of the authority of the General
Assembly and the UN Secretary General.
   If there is a North/South imbalance, it is at
the upper controlling General Assembly echelon
where the industrialised countries have little
power to sway a vote and thus they prefer both with
respect to economic and to political subject areas
to preserve the vapour of words and documents
rather than to create a strong controlling and
directing centre. The study by Jackson on the
non-aligned shows that over the last ten or so
years the non-aligned have voted much more with the
Soviet Union than with the United States; but
Jackson went to some lengths to point out:

> "Coincidence on the majority of issues with
> the Soviet position, is therefore not
> necessarily a measure of Soviet influence or
> control. For most NAM (non-aligned) members,
> it results in greater part from differences
> with US and other Western positions on
> specific issues and underlying post-colonial
> mistrust(apart from a group of outright
> Soviet supporters)."[1]

Indeed Tikhomirov for UNITAR [2] has shown how the
Pacific island countries, India and China vote more
with the US when the US votes yes, that is it
supports a resolution and the USSR opposes than the
reverse position, which demonstrates that the
issues are more important than where are the

superpower allegiances. Whether the bout of
dissatisfaction with the ultimate 'permanent
majority' of the developing countries in the
General Assembly and specialised agency assemblies
arising in the developed 'western' countries is
perhaps a more temporary phenomenon is an important
question. The 8 year period from 1973 following the
oil price rises was one where the developing
countries tried to show some political muscle in
their own interest. The debates and resolutions on
the New International Economic Order
(NIEO)[3]reflect this trend and the demands of NIEO
and the politicisation of debates has been one of
the main criticisms of those)[4] who reject the
legitimacy of the one country vote assemblies.
However, the world recession since 1979 has
increasingly sapped developing country economic
strength and NIEO is almost a dead issue in 1985.

Although decolonisation is almost ended, all
the very small states have joined the UN as full
members and are unlikely to want a lower status;
however the voting power of the mini-states is
unjustifiable in theory or practice. There is no
fair parallel between universal personal suffrage
in a single state and one-country-one-vote for all
states. Personal suffrage in a single state implied
that the vote of a poor man counted for the same as
a rich man; the parallel for countries is that the
income of a country should not determine the number
of its votes. It does not mean that a country of a
billion population should have the same number of
votes as a country having a population of less than
a million. The inequality of states is far greater
(in all dimensions) than the inequality of persons,
especially at birth. The 'inalienable' Rights of
Man ("a man°s a man for all that" - from Robert
Burns) do not extend to states. The basis of voting
in the General Assembly and its Committees is a
question of expediency not of inalienable rights.

Before looking at reform proposals again, it
should be stated as an axiom that no changes in
voting procedures which allowed the high level
institutions of the UN to legitimise their
decisions in the global community should be allowed
to diminish the search for concensus. In the
absence of a decision making procedure, the whole
emphasis has been thrown on the search for
concensus. This procedure allows just one country
to block progress, but it also produces an enormous
educative process, a concerned dialogue between
opposing parties, widespread participation in the

search for a compromise and a greater loyalty to
decisions made as a result. No new voting decision
procedure should increase the polarisation of the
blocks and destroy the participatory search for a
compromise. It should not be forgotten that the aim
is not for a strong elected government where power
changes hands between elections. Within the
existing Charter system of representation by
country, there can never be government rotating by
blocks; coalitions and compromises are required
permanently on all issues.

A UNITED NATIONS WHICH AVOIDS BOTH UNDUE
HETEROGENEITY AS WELL AS MONOLITHISM

It is more clear what reforms are not wanted than
what is wanted. An unduly heterogenious United
Nations proliferates agencies, units, programmes,
is impossible to control or coordinate, is
wastefully competitive, duplicating services and
eventually avoids the main issues. Also to be
avoided is a monolithic United Nations, top heavy
with a powerful bureaucracy under a central and
isolated control.
     The argument that most UN reforms will create
a monolithic UN System only holds because there is
not a voting and decision structure accepted by all
member countries. If the General Assembly could
pass a resolution by, for example, a majority or
two-thirds majority and its constitutional validity
was accepted even if it did not please all
participating governments, then the beginning of a
responsible secretariat or executive could be
constructed. The acceptable constitutional basis
for taking decisions in the General Assembly would
pass down to all lower level assemblies which
governed either sectoral or decentralised organs of
the System. Even the fear of supranationalism would
be greatly reduced by broad agreement on a voting
decsion structure. Power could be made responsible;
it is the fear of a strong irresponsible
bureaucracy which justifies the attacks on
monolithism; rather a weak uncontrolled structure
than an irresponsible controlled one. Far
preferable is a controlled responsible structure;
such would not be monolithic.
     Another essential component of a UN which was
not monolithic and was well planned and controlled
is a restriction on the possible zones of its
interventions. A powerful UN which confined itself
mainly to interstate disputes and kept a tight rein

on the areas of international law making which
might impact on national law would be more
acceptable than one which had unlimited rights to
intervene. For example the Charter only gave the
Security Council a limited right to intervene
against the wishes of a member state in the cases
of breaches of the peace. The only way to convince
member states that a powerful UN would not be
inconsistent with most capitalist or
socialist/communist regimes would be to exactly
circumscribe the areas of intervention. The most
vexed areas would be human rights and the
restraints against inviting assistance from
friendly states to control internal political
change. The supervision of treaties would have to
be tightened and to remain acceptable would have to
be phased. Initially human rights could be covered
by the same conventions as at present and only
countries that had signed would be subject to a
strengthened supervision machinery. In the case of
invitations to friendly states for armed
assistance, international law would only have any
impact when a system of collective security was put
in place. For some time to come that system would
have to omit the permanent members of the Security
Council who, in any case, would be unlikely to
require assistance from any other state.

However much it is possible to convince by
planning, coordination on the one side, or power
limitation, devolution and decentralisation on the
other, that responsiveness and people contact can
be preserved, the arguments will still count of
little value. If the policy direction is going to
continue to be given by an Assembly which is
dominated by countries which neither represent the
global balance of economic power, nor global
populations(in any easily recognisable manner), nor
the financial contributions to the System
(especially if the admittedly loaded voluntary
contributions are included), then the North and
West industrialised countries are going to be
reluctant to accept the Assembly's decision making
legitimacy. In the General Assembly, states
containing less than 12% of the population and less
than 5% of the worlds income could theoretically
muster a 2/3rds. majority.[5] A solution to the
problem of the legitimacy of the decisions of the
General Assembly will pave the way for all the
reforms of the System which will lead to its
greater relevancy and more efficient operation.The
question of perceived imbalances of power is the

priority issue and it is clear that institutional
reform cannot be tackled piecemeal.

It is of course no answer to say that the
permanent members dominate the Security Council
which in some way balances the General Assembly.
The Security Council does not touch upon economic
or development issues and the developing country
block now has almost the same veto power in that
body as the permanent members. The Security Council
is not the executive body of the General Assembly,
least of all in economic and development matters.

That the World Bank/IMF Group to some extent
balances off the power of the General Assembly is
also only partial answer; however this group is
not accepted by the General Assembly as some kind
of executive body, nor by the other UN agencies, so
the Group's power is isolated. Also the socialist
North and East are not sufficiently represented in
the World Bank/IMF Group so that the answer does
not lie in that direction.

To give legitimacy to the voted decisions of
the General Assembly is not a simple question of
restoring the balance lost when developing country
members became the overwhelming majority; that
majority is the principle balancing force between
the North/West and North/East.

WEIGHING THE POLITICS BEHIND THE OPTIONS FOR REFORM

There is some pressure for changes in the voting
structure of the General Assembly from developed
countries and some, from the developing countries,
for changes in the veto procedures of the Security
Council. A possibility of a trade between the two
groups on the two sets of reforms has been
proposed[6] but there has not so far been much
enthusiasm for reform, possibly because the
socialist East may not come out of such a trade
with any worthwhile gains.

The first main argument that the balance of UN
power is still currently not right and is likely to
grow worse is that at no time have the developed
countries been willing to accept real North/South
negotiations or major financial power in the one
country one vote assemblies, preferring to work
through the weighted voting 'Bretton Woods'
institutions of the World Bank/IMF group and GATT.
If these institutions are to play their full role
and receive global legitimacy for actions currently
only controlled by developed countries, then some
stronger links to the General Assembly have to be

made. The second argument is that all the
procedural points in which the developed countries
have managed to preserve de facto power in the
General Assembly and the specialised agencies will
be slowly eroded as at least some of the developing
countries grow in strength. The recession has
temporarily strengthened the developed countries in
the United Nations forums but there are reasons to
believe the relative advantage may not hold as some
of the developing countries adapt to the changed
circumstances. As time passes also, certainly
Japan and other major countries will refuse to be
excluded from the group of permanent members which
will open up the issue of the membership and power
of the Security Council. The issue of Security
Council membership can only be delayed as long as
the sequence of summits East and West followed by a
superpower summit is acceptable to all the
countries excluded.

The burning question is whether there are any
reforms which could receive the votes of both the
North/West and the North/East, maintain the balance
of voting power of the non-aligned countries and
continue to allow that situation to be regarded as
the norm. It is not sufficient to argue that one
only needs to wait until after some highly
influential governments have changed with the
democratic swing of the pendulum, although doing so
still may ease the passage of reform; waiting for
changes of government suggests that the reforms are
only of transient value whereas what is wanted is a
constitutional framework flexible and strong enough
that within it changes of government will not cause
the framework to crumble.

The constitutional vulnerability of the UN
System will always be precarious as long as its
power depends on the solidarity of governments
rather than direct elections. A period of detente
or a well preserved strong middle ground of
non-aligned countries can allow the System to
continue to function, basically as it is
constructed now, plus or minus some reforms to
improve efficiency. If the ideolgical battle
between the superpowers is regarded as the norm,
and either detente ends or the middle ground swings
or appears to swing from the point of view of one
or other superpower, then the whole System is under
attack. First the USSR and then the US in turn have
attempted either to limit the freedom of action of
the UN System or to attack its constitutional base

143

because the middle ground appeared to move towards the other side.

The ending of the ideological cold war more permanently than through temporary periods of detente mainly lies outside the influence of the United Nations, although the non-aligned could do more within the organisation to generate the international understanding to move the process along. Such programmes are likely to have only a relatively marginal effect in the short term but much more in the long term, especially if there is increasing freedom of information for the passage of UN literature. For example the UN University or UNESCO could be asked to promote and disseminate studies of government and organisation that can pose some practical paths in common towards the diminution of some of the most intractable of the global and national problems of the West and East. The organisational deficiencies that cause butter mountains and the Challenger disaster in the West and declining grain land productivity and the Tchernebyl disaster in the East would be worth comparing to find, isolate and illustrate the common factors. The nature of government greatly effects human rights, prevention of ecological damage and the militarisation of society. Although academic studies do not change the direction of powerful forces such as economic nationalism, when added to a dissemination process and aided by governments then their impact is greatly multiplied. It is not wishful thinking that the governments of the socialist East will aid such studies because they not only need to find ways out of their dilemmas but they have to convince a very wide number of party activists, regional and local political leaders. The more open the society the greater the need for information and education to replace discipline and command. The socialist East will clearly be moving in this direction and the point is that their governments may have come to understand that they have as much chance of winning ideological battles as the capitalist West if the problems of running a more open society with socialist goals can be better resolved. In these circumstances studies of common problems covering the relation between methods of government, administration, corporate systems and technology in the two societies may well be supported by the socialist East. There was in the 1970's a lot of work done in western academic circles and UNITAR on desired world order systems[7] and the limits of diversity whilst still preserving the decencies and preventing the disasters, but the level of the debate was very restricted and it must go very much wider to be of any real value. Oscar Schachter suggested using the UN University with its branches in different countries as well as standing regular seminars in the major cities of the world.

> "An important aspect of these seminar activities should be a broad participation of experts from a given country or region together with simultaneous relations with the governments of different countries."[8]

Even though it can be expected that the repercussions on the West will be as great as on the East, if the socialist East is not prepared to enter into the debate then there is no point in continuing with the studies programme. A debate has commenced as a result of the 1985 Geneva summit. The superpower heads of state can address each other by sattelite television, why not the UN Secretary General. By implication why could there not be other UN television material produced and by agreement with the national authorities broadcast to widen the debate. The West dare not refuse to enter into an open debate as such openness is their strongest argument. If the non-aligned countries took the initiative, as they too have a considerable interest in the outcome, then the socialist East might also agree. The moment may well be ripe to try and the Secretary General could put the issue squarely before the two superpower leaders and the rest of the international community. Although the practicable possibility of direct elections for the General Assembly are remote, it is worth speculating the impact that such elections might have on the socialist countries. There is much less fear that their own total vote would be swamped by the vote of the non-communist countries compared with the 1950's, but the Party hierarchy in the socialist East countries would ask whether directly elected representatives might not surrender too much of the democratic centralism on which the system depends. If at least initially it was only possible for a more powerful UN to intervene in a highly circumscribed manner, for the solutions of interstate disputes and to supervise treaties and conventions that each state had willingly ratified, then the socialist countries would not be under any threat to their systems. It could be said that the socialist countries have signed a number of treaties which they did not believe could be effectively supervised. One answer is that where supervision was to be strengthened appreciably a new treaty would be required. A second answer is that the socialist regimes will be more open because they not only need solutions but they know there is no monopoly on the answers from either side; we could only find out whether the socialist East would accept these arguments by experiment, that is after studies and debate.

A second line of defence in the long term objective of giving greater constitutional legitimacy to the UN General Assembly is indirect election of delegates by national legislatures. The socialist East would find no problem ensuring that representatives conformed on essential issues whilst having the extra dimension of coming from non-government assemblies. The problem would be on the side of the North/West; would they make the same criticism of the indirectly elected delegates as they have made of the trade union and employers representatives to the ILO tripartite system, that the socialist country representatives all vote the same way as the government. However valid the criticism, it would be a significant concession on the part of the socialist Eastern Bloc countries to accept the decisions of indirectly elected delegates as a basis of international law making and, apart from the propaganda points that may be scored by the North/Western group of countries, the socialist indirectly elected representatives should be accepted at their face value because a major step forward will have been made.

The importance of the non-aligned in the UN as a middle ground between the superpowers cannot be exaggerated. A great deal of effort has been exerted by the superpowers in the late 1970's and 1980's to win over more of the previously non-aligned to their own camp. The more successful are the superpowers in eliminating the number of genuinely non-aligned amongst the South, the greater the difficulty in giving any permanent legitimacy to the UN General Assembly without direct elections. Without a strong middle ground neither superpower will trust General Assembly decision making but their own actions are eroding any possibility for increasing that trust. The forces of ideological competition and military security leading the superpowers to increase the numbers of their supporters are stronger than

their motivation to work closer with the UN. Given
the debt crisis and the economic pressures
resulting from the recession, it is surprising
that many more countries in the South have not
become susceptible to political pressure.The
recent extreme steps taken by the United States
for example, to counter international terrorism
may be of long term significance in reinforcing
the political neutrality of the non-aligned.
Neither superpower likes to be dictated to by the
South, even in the name of the UN and
international law, especially as they fear it is a
law not just of the middle ground and moderation
but special pleading for a New International
Economic Order in their own interest. The
non-aligned must play the role of mediator in the
global battle of the titans but they cannot avoid
their own concerns. The dilemma of the non-aligned
in not being able to be moderators and promote
their own concerns at the same time has been
brilliantly analysed by Yoshikazu Sakamoto of
UNITAR:

> "As the East-West conflict began to recede
> and the North-South division has come to the
> fore, however, the value-neutral concept of
> the international system is no longer
> sufficient for the adequate achievement of
> the goals and objectives of the United
> Nations. Bridging the gap between North and
> South requires, not the termination of
> negative symetric interdependence but the
> realisation of positive asymetric
> interdependence. It calls for not
> dissociation but association of the parties
> in conflict."[9]

Either the arenas for peace and security are kept
as separate as possible from those which tackle
economic and development issues, with the balance
of power maintained by the South in the former and
the North in the latter, or the terms of the
North/South conflict have to be considerably
narrowed. One direction this logic leads is that
the non-aligned should be allowed a greater say in
the Security Council, even more so than they have
at present, whilst reducing their power to vote
economic changes for which they do not pay in the
economic forums of the UN, a very difficult
quid-pro-quo for all the parties to accept. A
second is that the debate on North/South issues
should be temporarily suspended to enable some

more permanent solutions to peace and security
problems to be found, with the South acting as
moderator, an unlikely scenario given the
heterogenity of the South and the economic
pressures upon them. A more hopeful third
alternative is that combined with moves towards
detente between the superpowers, some minimum
permanent bargain can be struck on global
North/South transfer payments and trade protection
policy. The political pressure for such a bargain
would come from the rest of the Northern countries
seeking to insure themselves against the
strengthening of superpower detente by building
more bridges to the non-aligned. It will be
appreciated that a reformed UN is a secure base
for not only the non-aligned countries in the case
of a long period of detente, but also for the
excluded countries of the North who may feel that
such an alliance may not be always in their
interest.

This chapter is dominated by the idea of
trying to find reform solutions which might be
acceptable to both superpowers. The question is
whether it is necessary to twist into contortions
in order to do this. Preserving the universality
of the UN System is clearly very important if it
is to be a forum for interstate problem solution.
However a UN of 159 member states is still a very
significant organisation. Even if either the
United States or all the North/East socialist
countries were to walk out, the organisation would
still represent a significant force. The gains
from a stronger reformed organisation capable of
effectiveness and control may be much more than
the losses from the leaving of some, albeit
powerful and influential members. The same members
may return after a period of reflection. The
question whether the financial loss from one or
other superpower leaving the organisation is
insupportable clearly influences consideration of
the issues. However, it has already been concluded
that the individual contributions of member states
in terms of their own budgets and national incomes
is relatively insignificant. The remaining
countries will naturally grumble at picking up the
bills left by departing countries but the real
cost is not likely to be large if all participate
and indeed the cost savings from the extra
efficiency from more effective control and less
duplication may largely compensate. If enough
countries are able to establish an effective and

148

responsive United Nations then, as it was seen to succeed, more of those who were doubtful would be won around, in much the same way as the European Economic Community has enlarged from the original six to the current twelve. If countries stayed only to prevent changes, then the possibility of reconstituting the United Nations under another banner should not be ruled out as a last counter response; contingency plans could be prepared as a tactical move to illustrate how it could be done without unacceptable disruption.

From a strategical point of view, when detente is in the air it would be sound to concentrate on peace and security issues and strengthen the role of the Security Council, with the Group of 9 members from the South playing a moderating and initiating role to move the process along, bringing as many of the non-superpower Northern members with them. When the air for detente is cold, the strategy should move to carve away the institutional setting for the North/South issue from that for peace and security; the aim would be to establish the ground rules for a first stage planetary bargain, perhaps covering North/South transfer payments and lasting for a defined period (say three years), which would go just sufficiently far as to allow the non-aligned countries to play during that period, a more significant moderating role on peace and security matters and not be regarded as biased parties to their recommendations in the seperate forums. The chances of achieving a first stage planetary bargain do not look at all promising but a clear strategy with modest first aims should assist. In all events the weight of initiative is thrown first on the non-aligned; by accepting some reduced power in a reformed General Assembly it opens up the way for General Assembly determined North/South negotiations. These, once achieved, would allow the non-aligned to act as moderators for collective security and detente. With some significant moves towards peace and security achieved in the Security Council, the non-aligned could switch back to their own concerns in the General Assembly and a second stage in the planetary bargain. This strategical framework could run parallel to UN reform efforts, concentrating in turn on the Security Council and then the General Assembly.

Conclusion

EXISTING SUGGESTIONS FOR GENERAL ASSEMBLY REFORM

Examples of suggestions for reforming the General Assembly or Economic and Social Council voting procedures are numerous.

Creating a special category of associate member states (the Colombian proposal) would delete the 'mini-states' from the voting majority of the developing countries. As most small states are full members already and small states value their membership, it would prove almost impossible to introduce. Most votes are decided by regional block leaders and contact men; mini-states do not influence the direction of voting, although they do bolster the numbers in the developing country block.

Decisions on important questions (perhaps budgetary questions or in particular committees) could be decided by two-thirds of members present, provided that these members represent two-thirds of world population and two-thirds of UN budgetary contributions (known after its inventor as the "Hudson Proposal"). This is a sensible suggestion because although, as it is currently formulated, it uses a budget criteria which approximates 'global economic power', this relationship is not inevitable. It would only be necessary to change the budget assessment and the decision limits set by the 'Hudson Proposal' alter accordingly. The second limit set by global population not only has a basis in rationality because it eliminates the effective power of mini-states to swing decisions but it is neutral between North and East although it would give the vote of China considerable influence. Another problem with the 'Hudson Proposal' is that lobbying becomes difficult and assessing voting outcomes requires computer calculations to know which way decisions may go. However pre-programmed mini-computers could provide instant results for all lobby work.

Choosing a weighting, whether it be in the plenary of the General Assembly or in the Fifth Committee(which governs System financing), requires subtlety. Weighted voting on budgetary matters is the condition in one of the United States proposals(the Kassebaum amendment) for relaxing the witholding of 20% of their UN assessment. However any formula chosen must eliminate permanent majorities and not so be weighted towards the powerful mixed economies of the North West as to nullify the voice of the

socialist East. Hanna Newcombe of the Dundas
Ontario Peace Research Institute produced data up
to the 28th session of the General Assembly which
shows what would have happened ceteris paribus if
different weighted voting proposals had been used
for each of the resolutions put to the vote over
this period[10]. It is clear that there is very
little difference between UN assessment and GNP as
a weighting factor and that if either is used it
will swing even simple majority decisions towards
the North West. Using population by itself does
not greatly change the existing voting pattern and
any logarithmic or non linear function only
increases the 'permanent majority'. The choice is
between an arithmetic function of the UN
assessment with a minimum floor of 3 votes(a
suggestion by Mano quoted by Newcombe) or a 1:1
ratio between population and UN assessment.
Whether the simple majority rule is used or a two
thirds one, perhaps initially, is a question of
confidence in the system chosen.

Table 6.1
    Alternative Weighted Voting Systems and their
    Impact on Majorities in a General Assembly
    Resolution 3103(xviii:Colonialism-Human
    Rights in Armed Conflicts)

Weighted Voting Systems	No Vote	Yes Vote	Ratio No/Yes
current simple majority	13	82	.15
population weighted	142	349	.41
GNP weighted	385	369	1.04
UN assessment	403	363	1.11
square root population	111	515	.22
UN assess.arith.funct. +floor 3 votes	314	447	.70
population+UN assessment	275	357	.77

An example was taken from the Newcombe data to
illustrate in Table 6.1 above how the different
weighting systems change the majority. Only the
current voting methods and the population and
square root of population weighted systems produced
a two thirds majority on this resolution. Voting
could be weighted by similar categories as used in
IFAD; each block has a number of votes and the
blocks determine the intra-block voting rule they
want in order to distribute their block votes. The
System already operates in blocks but is by no
means stable on all issues and countries would lose
their flexibility if they had to remain permanently

151

in one block for all votes. However one motive for
flexibility is to present a domestic posture and it
would be a considerable gain if block voting
removed incentives for time wasting speech making
of little real importance to the real issues under
discussion. The outcome would be more anonymous and
possibly therefore more rational. There would be
less political wrangling and politicisation of
technical debates. For example the work of the
Committee on Programme Coordination is highly
technical and its scarce time should be given over
to ensuring that planning matches priorities, that
agencies cooperate and eliminate duplication and
that programmes achieve their objectives. This is
not always the case. A start could be made by
introducing such a system into the Committees
before trying it in the plenary meetings.

A subsidiary organ with weighted voting can be
created where all resolutions must pass before
going to the plenary. The difference between this
suggestion and weighted voting in say the Fifth or
other Standing Committees is that the plenary could
not introduce proposals if the subsidiary organ had
not first passed them. Thus the subsidiary organs
created would have very considerable powers.

These detailed suggestions would only become
interesting and important when agreement had been
reached on the major political trade-offs. Initial
reform efforts should be concentrated on putting
together a balanced and phased package and if this
is not done, the above suggestions will remain
merely academic pipe dreams. Perhaps not even the
temporary crisis in the UN's finances can be solved
without such a balanced package and the 1986
difficulties in finding solutions are a good
illustration of this point. All the suggestions
have some flexibility built into them, the budget
assessment is open to amendment, the block voting
depends upon the actual number of votes to each
block and the number and grouping of the blocks and
the weighted voting in a subsidiary organ need not
be immutable. If there is a concensus for change
there is room for it without either the need to
amend the Charter or to break the organisation. The
suggestions made here illustrate the nature of such
a package which needs to be very clearly but
flexibly posed. The job of selected country
representatives and the Secretariat is to formulate
the concepts and bring about the required debates
at a time when the political climate is ripe.

THE AGENCIES HAVE TO SUBMIT TO UNITED NATIONS SYSTEM WIDE POLICY

If decision making forums and procedures were found at the level of the General Assembly and its Committees, then the control of System agencies and programmes could be tightened without favouring necessarily one or other political block. Once there is the possibility of control, the question of regionalisation ceases to be an alternative to control and becomes one of managerial efficiency. The issue of regionalisation ceases to burn.

There is little doubt in my mind that UN managerial efficiency would greatly increase with regionalisation. The problem of coordination would be forced downwards more and more to levels where decentralised group decision making replaces planning as a means of coordination. In fact it is probably the only rational way to handle a large number of complex technical subjects. Nevertheless even under a highly decentralised structure certain problems remain. First, there would still need to be high level planning and policy control. Second, regionalisation of itself may not innovate intersectoral solutions to many problems because even at the lower levels where group decision making can replace planning, the sectoral division of responsibility is as binding as at upper echelons. Innovative inter-sectoral programming would be a necessity. To prevent regions having their own inviolate sectoral frontiers, responsibilities could be carried into temporary programme divisions under programme managers where there was no pretence that frontiers are mutually exclusive. This does not annul the need for innovative inter-sectoral (or inter-programme) programming; it just softens up the programme managers' hard shell of resistance and shares around the expertise because within programme planning would itself be inter-sectoral.

The only major arguments against regionalisation of the System are political. First the balance of country blocks within each region becomes delicate if the regions have real power. However, much policy direction is maintained by the central organs, the regions would have major devolved responsibilities and hence power. Second, it would mean a gigantic upheaval of the existing system of agencies and the resistance could be expected to be horrendous. The opposition would not only come from the agencies themselves which have

talent in these kind of exercises but also from the
sectoral ministries of member countries. The fight
in all normal circumstances would not be worth
undertaking. One would lose and come away bruised
and beaten.

The recommendations in Chapter 4 would greatly
strengthen coordination and UN System policy
coherence, both at central and at country levels.
These are:

At Central Levels
- A coherent simultaneous System wide planning
  cycle would ensure that the controlling
  committees and commissions of the System would
  more easily be able to eliminate duplication
  and prioritise complementary programmes;
- Medium term plans must be shown with
  relatively detailed objectives and broad
  budget guidelines for each programme. In this
  way programmes will not supercede their laid
  down budgets which can be made to conform to
  policy priorities. Programmes will be asked to
  say what they intend to achieve in practical
  terms so that at the end of the Plan,
  evaluations can guide the next planning cycle.;
- The Director-General for Development must be
  the person responsible within the UN System
  for ensuring high level coordination and
  policy planning for all agencies in the area
  of developent. He would use the Committee on
  Programme Coordination, the ACC and the
  regular meetings of Agency governing bodies to
  exercise his powers of coordination, supported
  by his own office staff and that of the DIESA;
- The Department of Development would
  considerably prune some of its lower priority
  technical cooperation support services and
  with the Regional Commissions concentrate on
  support for multi-sectoral programming;
- The Administrator of UNDP would be directly
  under the Director-General for Development.
  The ability to make such a change would wholly
  depend on the reforms within the General
  Assembly which would return to the General
  Assembly its controlling functions over the
  whole System. Without these reforms in the
  General Assembly, the reccomendations would
  place UNDP's voluntary funds totally under the
  control of the recipient countries which
  currently is not acceptable to the donors;

- Regular meetings of representatives of governing bodies of agencies in relation to the Committee on Programme Coordination to give a firm lead and control to policy planning.

At Country Levels
- Resident Coordinators will become the focal points for a new system of technical cooperation supporting UN agreed policies;
- A clear statement every 4-6 years of UN System policies will be made for each country by the national Ministry of Planning in cooperation with the UN/UNDP and the agencies including the World Bank Group. This one document will be binding on all UN System agencies and also be an authoritative guideline for bilateral agencies. This document in draft will form the basis for high level dialogue between the UN System secretariats and government and when finalised will be used to prepare the detailed country programme of aid and technical cooperation;
- Joint inter-agency/government programming exercises will be supported by the regional commissions specifically concentrating on the interdisciplinary and intersectoral approaches and to assist in the identification of UN agency and also where possible bilateral agency contributions. The results of these exercises will be incorporated into the country planning and programming cycle, that is, the high level policy paper and the detailed country programme;
- A regular simultaneous programming cycle will be used by all UN agencies linked to a System wide country programme of aid and technical cooperation, as far as possible including the bilateral agency contributions. Within the programming cycle will be a regular calendar of government/bilateral agency /UN System/dialogue.The dialogues with government by high level teams followed by programming teams can be the same dialogue that takes place with governments as part of global economic management, recommended in Chapter 3. The calendar of meetings would include bi-annual negotiations which were confined to short-term monetary and fiscal adjustments as well as the more medium term dialogue on

Conclusion

development priorities and structural
adjustments.

PLAUSIBLE REFORM OPTIONS

The plausible reform options are influenced by
whether there is a reform of the Charter implied. A
major blockage on Charter reform in general is that
any change in the Charter to improve consideration
of economic and development questions would also
lend force to the arguments for Charter reform
which might diminish the power of the existing
permanent members of the Security Council[11],
although it has been argued earlier that some kind
of trade off over these two issues poses the
greatest chance for a permanent solution to the
problem of the reform of the UN. There are three
kinds of reform proposals. Those which are really
more than reforms and are wholesale restructuring
based on a completely different theoretical basis.
Second are the reforms which involve amending the
Charter and third are the reforms, however radical,
within the existing Charter. The three case studies
and the recommendations here are based on the third
and last species of reform, not because of any
inherent belief in them but because it is the most
plausible option here and now. Some examples of all
three types are given below:

Theoretically Different Basis for a UN

Most current discussions about UN reform are very
narrowly based with only a very short time
horizon. The problems are so immediate that
concerns are for the here and now. Although not
much time in this book has been devoted to very
radical proposals mainly because they have no
chance of receiving sufficient support,
nevertheless it would be unwise to lose sight of
long term objectives. What might be some long term
objectives?
    A UN with decision making powers is required
but covering a restricted area so that there was
not unnecessary interference in the affairs of
countries, localities and peoples. The UN should
thus be concerned more to make international law
governing interstate relations than it would to set
standards for national law making; it would set
such standards for example in human rights but it
would have to be prepared, following on the
assumption of decision making powers, initially to
take a restrained attitude in this area. In the

156

long run the ideological battle between communism
and capitalism may soften and the idea of applying
universal standards in a number of sensitive areas,
such as liberty of association, or basic minimum
needs may not carry the connotations or practical
implications that they do at the present time.
Until then, restraints on international law making
would need to be much greater than the areas
currently allowed for resolutions and conventions.

The General Assembly would become a
legislature and would thus have to be made more
responsible and accountable than is currently
possible with indirect representatives from
governments. Such a degree of responsibility would
entail some kind of direct election. As happened
when the European Parliament was created, a first
step was to have representatives indirectly elected
by national legislatures. Instead of relying on a
series of large committees to sift legislation or
resolutions, the General Assembly would require an
executive of nominated or indirectly elected
ministers or commissioners. If it was desired to
keep the balance of power different for peace and
security issues relative to economic and
development issues then not only is the Security
Council maintained but so is the Economic and
Social Council, reducing the size and increasing
the power of the latter. The extent of the
responsibility of these two executive bodies to the
General Assembly would depend on what fund raising
functions the elected members disposed, either from
sources independent of governments or as a result
of their ability to influence national legislators.

Apart from the funds required for the
Secretariat and funded programmmes of research and
statistics, which are relatively small, the real
expenditures of a decision taking UN would be in
peace and security matters, mainly peace-keeping
forces and only very rarely enforcement actions, as
well as for economic and social development. In
both these areas a return to multilateralism will
depend upon confidence building through the new and
more deliberate machinery. With increasing
confidence, the possibility of replenishment of the
World Bank IDA, IFAD, UNEP, UNDP and UNICEF grant
and low interest loan facilities, and other
assisted financing would be achieved through a form
of global assessment and perhaps even through UN
automatic funding sources such as the suspended
'Sea Bed Authority'.

Conclusion

Currently the ILO is the nearest that the UN
comes to having a functional assembly, with its
tripartite representatives from governments,
employers and workers. The option would be open to
replace the ILO by a new functional assembly,
having as well representatives from the UN
accredited NGO's, or to enlarge the role of the NGO
meetings which take place before many of the
assemblies of the UN and the specialised agencies.
Resolutions agreed by the functional assemblies
might pass, for example, the General Assembly with
a lesser majority than two thirds or the functional
assembly might have a right to propose amendments
and under certain circumstances to delay the
passage of decisions of the General Assembly or its
Committees.

If the idea of a directly elected General
Assembly appears far fetched, it is only necessary
to consider that a directly elected European
Parliament has already been established. The fact
that the Parliament has very little power is highly
relevant but that it is there at all is tangible
evidence that not every advance in politics is
wholly predictable from a hard realistic appraisal
of the facts. Whatever the future of the other
suggestions above, the idea of a directly elected
General Assembly should not be allowed to die and
some long term principles on which a start could be
made is appropriate even now. The ideas above
should be taken as examples; when radical proposals
of that nature are opened up, the true list is as
long as one wants to make it but of little
practical value unless linked to a particular
approach.

Charter Reforms

If it is possible to envisage reforms of the UN
Charter but not initially to create a whole new
basis for a UN, what would be the principle
recommendations. For the General Assembly the issue
is to move more power back to the countries from
which concessions on global economic policies and
major development funds must be wrung by a system
of weighted voting in the plenary or in all or some
of the main Committees. A system of weighting which
grouped votes into regional blocks would allow the
Assembly to concentrate on essentials and keep
undue politicisation out of the debates. Another
possibility is to allot special associate status to
'mini-states'but this suggestion is not

attractive because it would give offence without
achieving objectives.

With really effective control over the
economic and development functions of the United
Nations System emanating from the General Assembly,
there would not be the same need for a cumbersome
Economic and Social Council. A very much smaller
executive type body is required to orchestrate the
System policy coordination in place of the current
Committee on Programme Coordination as well as to
guide at a high level the crucial packages of
economic, trade and development bargaining and
negotiating sessions that are allocated to the
lower level agencies. This reformed Economic and
Social Council would continue to act under a wide
mandate from the General Assembly but its members
could be government Ministers or Commissioners.
Part of the mandate of the reformed Council would
be the duty to approve the budget of all the
agencies. Another crucial power would, with the
Secretary General of the UN, to approve the
appointments of all the Agency executive heads.
These combined powers would place the reformed
Council and the Secretary General at the centre of
the spiders web.

An effective controlling executive Economic
and Social Council is necessary whether or not
there is a major reform of the system of agencies.
It is not in my opinion feasible to abolish the
current agencies and allocate them to a new
decentralised regional structure. This is one
option that would clearly be considered but the
issue would occupy much more time and effort than
the results would justify. However once the reforms
in the General Assembly and Economic and Social
Council had been put in place, it would then be
timely to see whether the agencies could be wrought
into an effective and responsible system. If the
answer was then in the negative, the issue of
regionalisation could be taken up again.

If Charter reform of the Security Council was
a genuine option arising out of the high level
bargain which allowed the reform of the General
Assembly voting rules, then the options would
indeed need to be considered with some care.
Increasing the number of permanent members of the
Security Council would not allow any more positive
role for the Council; it would only increase the
already far too wide negative blocking powers.
Because attitudes may well be changing on the role
of permanent members and the veto, various ideas

should be canvassed. Outright abolition of the veto
and therefore permanent member status is probably
still unacceptable at any level of bargaining
stance. New decision rules could be substituted,
for example an affirmative vote of at least nine
members (with/or without the affirmative vote of at
least three permanent members), perhaps limited to
ending armed conflict. If the decision rules were
not effectively changed, then the better solution
is to rely on trying to gain agreement for a
Security Council Commission, established within the
Charter which would be required in all
circumstances as an executive body. In the absence
of a Security Council Commission which would open
the way for peace-keeping ground rules to be set by
the Security Council, it is necessary to write into
the Charter a minimum framework for peace-keeping
activities to allow them to be organised and
funded effectively.

Reforms Within the Charter

If the object is to achieve an initial global
bargain between East/West and North/South, then the
same objectives can be sought but somewhat weaker
than with Charter reform. The requirement for
weighted voting is weakened if it is restricted to
subsidiary committees rather than the plenary body
but the establishment of subsidiary Commissions is
allowable under the Charter and would be required
in all events. However setting up a new Economic
Commission or Council without doing something about
the existing Economic and Social Council(ECOSOC) is
awkward. Radical restructuring of ECOSOC is
necessary under all scenarios; if ECOSOC simply was
restrained in function or strangled slowly, it
would bring the UN into disrepute. The same
argument justifies Charter reform rather than some
of the methods below because it treats the public
and member states as mature adults instead of
solving problems over their heads by subterfuge.
     To encourage the North/West to cooperate in
the General Assembly, certain responsibilities,
such as the UN budget could be passed to a
committee, which itself was given one of the
different forms of weighted voting. Additionally
and stronger still would be to establish an
Economic Commission or Council having
(Commissioner) members indirectly elected or
nominated by permanent members and regional blocks.
A weaker alternative would be to bring together

existing bodies (World Bank groups/GATT and UNCTAD
Trade and Development Board) into a 'Forum' to
negotiate relevant decisions. Within the Charter,
it is also possible to bring the UNDP and other
specialised agency budgets and planning procedures
more under the control of the Secretary-General.
    Establishing a Security Council Commission as
recommended in Chapter 5 is open without Charter
reform. An alternative would be to increase the
range of questions in the Security Council
considered as procedural (i.e. all Charter Chapter
VI questions). However such a solution lacks
sufficient subtlety to gain support; it virtually
abolishes the veto over the range of issues that
the superpowers would like it retained.
    A possible basic package in the third group of
reforms, not requiring reform of the Charter, are
those wanted more by the industrialised West (A) as
against those wanted more by the South (B) with
each subject to conditions required by the
socialist East (the COMCOM block).

A = 1. Weighted voting in the Fifth Committee of
        the General Assembly and any Forum where
        decisions would be made on global economic
        policy and development funding;
    2. Fifth Committee power over specialised
        agency plans and budgets;
B = 1. A negotiating Forum with greater (COMCOM
        participation) where genuine North/South
        negotiations would be assured of taking
        place;
    2. Peaceful disputes settlement Commission
        over which the veto was less subject (and
        which did not initially attempt
        jurisdiction over the Permanent Members).

It is not difficult to make holes in any package,
including this one. If the General Assembly voted
down the Fifth Committee decisions, it would
nullify all progress and Charter reform would be
necessary. In this event the argument that the
specialised agencies were more efficient and
evolving faster than the UN might hold and there
was no effective control to be exerted. Such a
solution is only a last resort if it is quite
impossible to create a form of UN planning and
control which has the broad based consent of all
member states.
    It would take Charter reform to replace ECOSOC
with an economic council (as proposed by Bertrand);
if this was possible, the concept of a tier of

commissioners is appropriate in the economic sphere
as well as suggested here in the political. The
Forum suggestion is a second best solution
predicated on the low probability of charter
reform. The concept of the tier of commisioners
should not be underestimated. The precedent in the
Joint Inspection Unit and the International Civil
Service Commission for the UN is less important
than their example in the European Economic
Community. They stand midway between the political
assemblies of state representatives and the
secretariat. They would be the nascent executive of
the UN System. From the political side, the
Security Council is its own legislature (it is not
related to the General Assembly as executive to
legislature). From the economic side, at the
moment, there is nothing remotely resembling an
executive (with the exception of the Bank Group who
carry the role, but not the title to the role).

ARE WE HEADING TOWARDS OR EVEN AIMING AT SUPRANATIONALITY?

The weaknesses of the organisaton combined with the
lack of willingness to strengthen it does not lend
much force to the argument that there is much
tendency towards supranationality. Yet as with most
forces, there is some other force pushing the
opposite way; the steady build up of international
law, codes of conduct and international action,
carries elements of supranational authority. The
line between an 'authority' given by an
intergovernmental council and one given by a
supranational council needs clarification.

Intergovernmental	Supranational
– cannot interfere against the will of a member (state)	– can take decisions against the will of member (states)
– decisions taken by indirectly elected representatives of member (states)	– decisions taken by directly elected representatives

Examine the first row; first the Security Council
has the Charter powers to interfere under Chapter
VII, 'Breaches of the Peace' although the power has
been seldom used because some members do not want
to acknowledge the supranational nature of the
authority. This point is well appreciated. Less

well acknowledged is the binding nature of
decisions taken in intergovernmental organisations,
whether taken by concensus or some majority
decision frame. Nothing (except chapter VII) can be
voted against the will of a member state but if the
member state does once vote for some action, it is
then bound and every representation of that
commitment is an exertion of supranational
authority. For example, if the IAEA has
verification inspectors and a state accepts
verification, then it has willed the ends by
intergovernmental decision and the means by
supranational ones, the latter being contained
within the former for as long as the treaty or
agreement is accepted as not directly abrogated. If
there are many such agreements, the sum totality of
them comes almost to the boundaries of where a
limited power supranational authority would be. The
result could be the same. There are many such
decisions, from willingness to accept peace-keeping
forces, treaty verification, and acceptance of
human rights commissioners studies, to acceptance
of principles and global policies of technical
cooperation. Every time a WHO officer tactfully but
forcefully reminds a minister of health of his
government's commitment to primary health care
whenever more priority or WHO's own funds, are
being used for urban hospitals, the strength of his
representation stems from the (supranational)
authority of the original World Health Assembly
decision.

   Examine the second row; the authority derived
from the directly elected representatives is
entirely separate from the authority derived from a
government representative and stands above the
government representative. Where there is directly
elected representation not only the means are
supranational but also the ends; the higher level
authority is supranational. Even a general assembly
composed of representatives of national
legislatures rather than national governments would
have a higher supranational element in the setting
of objectives. This is the most important element
of supranationality because it is concerned with
responsiveness and responsibility. A secretariat,
Commissioners or IMF/Central Bank, to whom power is
delegated should not be without an added element of
greater responsibility. Governments who are so far
unwilling to add the element of responsibility are
therefore rightly also reluctant to abrogate the
power.

Conclusion

    As can be seen from the above discussion, the simple question of supranationality, or intergovernmental authority,[12] hides more complex issues. The real question is, from whence stems the right to intervene of an international authority, is it from an agreed policy or treaty delegated to a secretariat or executive, or does it come from an assembly with more, rather than less, responsiveness and responsibility.

    A responsible supranational UN is worth placing as a long term goal. What is implied by this conclusion:

1.   a General Assembly elected by representatives who are not the government (i.e., either direct election by the people or by national legislatures);
2.   clear definition of the boundaries of decision making in the General Assembly to preserve national and local autonomy;
3.   a choice of voting structure (proportional representation) in the General Assembly which eliminated permanent majorities and ensured dialogue, negotiation and compromise rather than 'strong government' in the solution of international problems;
4.   Some method, possibly a strengthened human rights commission or a linked NGO council which helped to keep the balance between, on the one side, universal principles and decisions and, on the other, local culture, tradition and minority rights.

If the above four principles were accepted, although they were not built into the immediate goals of reform, they could serve to plot a programme of work and public education on the future of the UN. The sooner the public is given some broadly accepted long term goals, the sooner can its influence be brought to bear to telescope the long term towards the present. In the short term, the most important contribution to the reform of the UN is to find an acceptable voting formula in the General Assembly which allows real control over the System. In the long run, only directly elected General Assembly representatives can legitimise the decisions taken and tame the squabbling that will arise in the medium term over the voting system chosen.

    The financial and funding crisis of the UN is derived wholly from the lack of confidence in the

unweighted voting of the General Assembly and
Economic and Social Council. Solutions in terms of
stricter payment of dues, special funds for special
purposes, the balance of voluntary funds over
assessment funds and automatic funding sources, are
easy to denote, but if the will is missing, are
impossible to agree in practice. There is no point
in investigating further the theory of UN funding,
if the basic reforms are not carried through; with
the reforms, the talking can be to some purpose.

FEASIBLE PATHWAYS

If an international conference gave its blessing to
a calendar of reform it would have some value in
educating public opinion. In making the calendar
the optimum option is to create certain acceptable
'trade-offs' among the blocks and move forward a
package at a time. A second option is to push
forward where one can and use the imbalances set up
to gain acceptance for its partner reform in the
package. A possible time frame is indicated in
figure 6.2. In the timetable shown, balances are
maintained vertically but some imbalance remaining
is only corrected in the following period. Any
actual dates would be meaningless at this stage.
    It should be appreciated that only the most
crucial reforms are indicated in figure 6.2,
reforms which are the key to all the subsidiary
changes necessary to make the UN function better.
With the long term targets in view, there may be
greater acceptance of unpalatable, temporary or
medium term solutions. That is why even if the
degree of commitment behind the long term is less
than for the short term, the whole should be
attempted to be explained and negotiated as a
package. The idea of putting together a mixed
package has worked very well for the EEC and the UN
can usefully institutionalise their successful
example.

RAISING PUBLIC CONSCIOUSNESS AND PUTTING THE
PROCESS OF REFORM IN MOTION

The process chosen should seek to widen the public
debate and reassure fears at the same time. The
issues handled by the UN are so highly suited to
the communications technological revolution, that
every use should be made of it in putting the
messages across. The institutions of the UN and
such of the specialised agencies who value their UN

Figure 6.2: A Possible Timeframe for Reforms

Time Institution Area	Short	Medium	Long
General Assembly	Commission on Weighted Voting	Weighted Voting in G.Assemble	Direct or Indirect Voting for G.Assembley
Econ/Fin/Develop	Forum; stronger planning controls	Amalgamation UNCTAD/GATT (ITO); Joint Executive for IMF/World Bank Group; Economic Commission	Economic Council
Security/ Disarmament	Commission (Third World disputes)	Mandate to Commission expanded	Ending of Permanent Member States

relationship could be also mobilised to assist in widening the debate.
A possible process framework might be:

1. A resolution tabled in the General Assembly outlines the objectives and early stages of the process of debate;
2. An expert committee draws up questionnaires and briefing notes for Regional Commissions, NGOs, specialised agencies, block country groups and other selected organisations;
3. A special effort will be made to mobilise the views of the developing country universities through the UN University to counter the tendency in the past for the North to overweight their intellectual input into international conferences;
4. The public debate on the questions is orchestrated by UN public information services;
5. Existing scheduled functional and regional conferences of the participating organisations will be asked to debate the questions ending with written submissions;
6. UN Expert Committee supported by the Secretariat writes the keynote conference papers with each major viewpoint and their solution options;
7. The Secretariat undertakes a diplomatic shuffle to narrow down the block differences and to attempt to put together one or more acceptable packages;
8. A General Conference is held in two halves; the first narrows down the major policy differences latent within the packages of reform so that a summit meeting of world leaders who attend the conference for this halfway stage can cut through the divisive issues. The second half will concern itself in tracing out the implications of the decisions taken;
9. Ratification by member states will either be a formality or the process described above will have failed in major part, although as a last resort there is the option to minimally sacrifice the universality of the organisation for greatly increased effectiveness.

There are headaches in each of the stages above. A lot of thought for example, has to go into how the

Conclusion

General Conference handles negotiations which lead
to agreement on the major policy issues; it will
be unfortunately too easy to push off important
issues to the second half of the Conference, after
the world leaders have departed, leaving some
irreconcilable problems which will frustrate the
second half of the Conference.
     The ability to amend the Charter is very
limited given the difficulty of obtaining the
agreement of all the permanent members. Reform
efforts should be conscious of a greater need for
flexibility in a world that is changing more and
more rapidly. The UN Charter needs to be a fixed
point as governments come and go but it has to
reflect the major power realities within a long
time trend, inflexible in response to short term
crises and flexible in the long term to absorb
changes in the global balance of power. It will be
important to remove from the Charter the amendment
clauses which place into the hands of those whose
power is perhaps waning the ability to prevent any
changes in the interest of those who are growing
more influential. The Charter should always
maintain a balance between power and equity; to
some extent a weighted voting system based on
population and UN assessment(or GNP) enshrines
this balance whilst allowing an in-built
flexibility to accomodate relative changes in the
power variable(the UN assessment).In the long
term equity can only be maintained by, at the
minimum, indirect elections for the General
Assembly and ideally direct elections. Bringing
peoples and governments to such a point will
require the skillful efforts of all those who
believe in global order and co-operation and even
then it may take a major world crisis to effect
the desired changes in attitudes. One point is
certain; the UN today is rarely allowed to be
effective in the areas of real importance in peace
and security, global economic management,
environment protection and development and as the
problems grow it is of less and less importance.
The world is at the mercy of unbalanced
competitive powers checked by only the limited
moral force of the UN System. At some time on the
downward curve towards crisis, the change in
attitudes will take place. It would be wise to
prepare well in advance for such an eventuality.
At the last resort the peoples of countries who
are resolved to work for international law and
co-operation can build their own UN with an open

door to those who may later find it in their best
interest to join. The disruption would be very
great but the cost of political and bureaucratic
time lost must be offset against the possible
lives saved, employment created and environment
protected. Maybe the threat of proceeding alone
without the reluctant members may prove
sufficient. Planning should be to minimise
failure; any forecast of the high probability of
failure should not deter because what other
untried acceptable alternatives are there?

Notes to Chapter 6.

1. Jackson R.L.-"The Non-aligned , the UN and
    the Superpowers", Council on Foriegn
    Relations, Praeger, 1983, page 140.
2. Tikhomirov V.B.-"Quantitative Analysis of
    Voting Behaviour in the General
    Assembly",UNITAR Policy and Efficacy Studies
    No 2 1981, see figures 24 and 25 on pages 44
    and 45.
3. 6th Special Session of the General Assembly
    1974 (Res. 3201 and 3202, S-VI).
4. Ibid. Heritage Foundation, 'A World without a
    UN'.
5. Newcombe H.-"Nations on Record",1975;
                -"Alternative Pasts",1983.
    Peace Research Institute, Dundas, Ontario.
6. Evidence before the US Congress hearing on
    "United Nations Reform" Committee on Foreign
    Relations. October 26 1979, Washington 1980.
7. The World Order Model Project series of books
    was sponsored by the Institute for World
    Order. The series was edited by S. Mendlovitz
    who also contributed "On the Creation of a
    Just World Order: Preferred Worlds for the
    1990's", published in New York by the Free
    press and in Europe by the North Holland
    Publishing Co.,1977. Other books in the
    series are by Ranji Kothari, Ali Mazuri,
    Richard Falk, John Galtung and Louis Beres.
    The work in UNITAR has been sponsored by
    Philip de Seynes; there was unfortunately a
    shift away from the theme of presenting
    alternative preferred options and policy
    implications to concentrate on the trend
    predictions of the future in the UNITAR
    studies. See for example the debate which
    raises this theme in, UNITAR-"The United

Nations and the Future", Proceedings of a
conference in Moscow, 1974, published in
Moscow in 1976.

8.   Ibid, UNITAR, p.427.
9.   Ibid, UNITAR, p.208.
10. Ibid, Newcombe, both references.
11. An argument used in "Renninger J.P. - 'ECOSOC
     : Options for Reform", UNITAR - E.81 XV PE/4,
     1981.
12. Some of these issues are tackled in Evan
     Luard's Chapter of Hedley Bull (Editor),
     "The Right to Intervene" Oxford, 1984.

Annex 1

ROUGH COSTING OF THE WORK OF THE SECURITY COUNCIL
COMMISSION

1.   Commission

     Includes salaries and costs for 15
     commissioners, 21 professional staff and 33
     general service staff.

2.   Factfinding

2.1 Strengthening RRUNDP's will require about 50
     assistant RRs located in understaffed offices.

2.2 20m/m consultant missions per year x $10,000
     per m/m

2.3 Phase I as indicated in 83.IX.3

3.   Observer Forces

     1 new force every 3 years lasting 10 years =
     22 case years over the 10 years x $3 million
     per case year divided by 10 = $7 million p.a.

4.   Peacekeeping Forces

     1 new force every 2 years lasting 8 years =
     28 case years over the 10 years x $50 million
     per case year divided by 10 = 140 million p.a.

5.   Economic Sanctions

     Includes UN contribution to aid national
     administrations and excludes any attempt to
     compensate for losses by countries
     participating in the sanctions.

     1 case every 3 years lasting 5 years = 14
     case years over the 10 years x $20 million
     per case year, divided by 10 = $28 million
     p.a.

6.   Enforcement Cases

    1 case every 3 years lasting 2 years = 7 case
    years over the 10 years x $130 million per
    case year, divided by 10 = $91 million p.a.

7.   UN Contribution to Standby Forces

    7.1 5000 troops on 2 weeks standby at $8per
        day.

    7.2 Approximately $200 million of equipment
        and supplies stockpiled, regularly turned
        over and maintained.

Sources: H. Wiseman – "Peace-keeping", Pergamon
                Press, 1983, Appendix
            D. Wainhouse – "International
                peace-keeping at the Cross
                Roads", John Hopkins, 1973
            J.G. Stoessinger, et al,-"Financing of
                the United Nations System",
                Brookings,Washington, 1964.

172

DRAFT COLLECTIVE SECURITY AND DISARMAMENT
AGREEMENT

1.General

1.1. The Collective Security and Disarmament
Agreement insures the signatory country
against both direct and indirect external
aggression.

1.2. In return for guarantees by the Commission of
the Security Council(hereafter called the
"Commission"), the signatory state will
undertake phased disarmament according to a
defined programme (annex A to this
Agreement). Apart from requests made to the
Commission under this Agreement for
assistance to resist aggression, the
signatory state is enjoined to refrain from
requesting or making use of armed forces
belonging to another state for defence
against internal dissent or external
aggression. This Agreement takes precedence
over all other mutual defence agreements or
treaties to which the signatory state is or
may become party.

1.3. The Agreement has an initial phase of 8 years
duration, after which it will become final,
unless the signatory country exercises its
option to withdraw (clause 2.3 below).

2.Collective Security

2.1. The Commission will undertake to mobilise
such armed forces in defence of the signatory
state against aggression as circumstances
require. These forces will be made up from
specified countries (named in Annex B to this
Agreement) and will be deployed at specified
intervals (as indicated in Annex C). At any
time the Commission may decide these forces
may be substituted for by a regular
contingent of United Nations forces.

2.2. This Agreement becomes operative immediately
upon signature. Collective security forces
can be drawn upon following three seperate
procedures:

Annex 2

(i)   Collective security forces can be called upon
      at any time by the signatory country, even if
      there is no proven aggression and the forces
      are to act in a peace-keeping role and are to
      be stationed within the territory of the
      signatory country. In this case, the
      signatory state will reimburse the United
      Nations the budgeted costs of the operation
      (cost definitions are presented in paragraph
      7 below).

(ii) Direct armed aggression (category i in
      paragraph 3 below) will be immediately
      notified to the Commission and then verified
      by it. Within two weeks from notification,
      the first agreed contingent(specified in
      Annex C), will be dispatched to the signatory
      country with temporary pacification
      objectives. Depending on the urgency of the
      position, new objectives will be drawn up by
      the Commission with the concurrence of the
      signatory country within one month of the
      dispatch of the first contingent. The costs
      of the collective security intervention to
      repel armed aggression will be attributable
      to the "Special Collective Security
      Contribution" indicated in paragraph 7 below.
      Collective security forces under i above can
      become forces under procedure ii once direct
      armed aggression has been verified.

iii) Collective security forces made available
      under this third procedure are to support
      "Non-military Sanctions", furthur defined in
      paragraph 7 below. Non-military sanctions
      will be decided upon by the Commission as a
      response to "Indirect Aggression"(defined in
      category ii in the classification of
      "Aggression" given in paragraph 3 below). The
      costs of the armed forces support in this
      procedure will be apportioned, as will all
      support costs for non-military sanctions,
      according to the normal United Nations
      formulae.

2.3. At the end of the 8th. year, this agreement
      will be jointly reviewed by the signatory
      country and the Commission and the signatory
      country is at liberty to withdraw and hence
      to nullify the Agreement before it becomes
      final at the commencement of the 9th. year.
      The Commission can only withdraw at this time
      if the review demonstrates significant
      violations of the Agreement.

3.Aggression

3.1. Acts of aggression under which this Agreement can be invoked are divided and defined under two group headings:

(i)<u>Direct Armed Agression</u>
This group covers armed intervention by another state or by means of the agency of a third party state which allows its territory to be used for such a purpose and the sending of armed bands or mercenaries in such numbers as could result in the violent overthrow of the regime.

(ii)<u>Indirect Aggression</u>
This group covers the organising, instigating, assisting or participating in acts of civil strife or terrorist acts and those acts of economic coercion of such severity that they could (excluding remedial aid tendered),lead to the violent overthrow of the regime of the signatory state, or reduce that state to a position of a satellite, or significantly threaten the territorial integrity and political independence of that state.

4.Disarmament

4.1. The phased disarmament programme (annex A to the Agreement), excludes police under civil control and such para-military forces as are allowed for in the Agreement (under annex D).

4.2. The signatory state agrees to mantain the scheduled programme of disarmament and to accept the verification by the Commission of compliance.

4.3. Disarmament levels will be verified using both of the following criteria:

(i) the proportion of the population of working age in the armed forces. The "armed forces" can exclude police and any force allocated to the United Nations for collective security, but will include the allowed for para-military forces.

ii) proportion of the Gross National Product, or total public sector expenditure, spent on defence; the choice between these two indicators can be made by the signatory state. Reference norms for the above

indicators have been set by the Commission
(and are shown in annex E). Deviations from
these norms, both to set final targets and to
allow for variations in phasing, will be
allowed(see paragraph 4.5. below). Current
or base levels for the indicators will be
agreed by the Commission and the signatory
state. The reference norms written into this
Agreement must be adjusted by the Commission
for all such collective sescurity agreements
and not for any selected group of agreements.
Adjustment to reference norms can only be
made at periodic intervals of five years,
commencing with the establishment year of the
Commission.

4.4. The phased programme of disarmament in the
Agreement(Annex A) covers three periods of
four years, twelve years in all. By the end
of the twelth year disarmament will have
reached a level commensurate with the full
working of collective security provisions as
they relate to the estimated long term
security position of the signatory state.

4.5. Deviations above the level of the reference
norms will be allowed by the Commission to
cover both temporary and longer term
exceptional circumstances. Deviations from
the reference norms should be limited to the
following justifications:

(i) exceptional long land boundaries along which
on at least one side population density is
relatively high.

(ii) history of frontier disputes over named
lengths of frontier.

(iii)history of tribal or racial disputes crossing
frontiers.

4.6. The allowable deviation from the reference
norms may be adjusted by mutual arrangement
between the parties to the Agreement at the
end of the 8th.year, before the Agreement
becomes final.

4.7. An example disarmament programme would be
laid out in the Agreement, as table annex 2.1.

Table Annex 2

Disarmament Programme

Disarmament Phasing	base period	reference norm	plus country deviation	Three phased programme		
				end 4 years	end 8 years	end 12 years
armed forces as % working population	5.2	1.0	1.1	4.0	2.5	1.1
defence expenditure % G.N.P.	4.5	0.8	0.9	3.0	1.5	0.9
defence expenditure % public sector expenditure	12.5	2.6	2.8	9.0	4.5	2.8

Annex 2

5.Signatory Country Forces Allocated to United Nations

5.1. Forces allocated to United Nations collective security by the signatory state are excluded from the programme of disarmament.

5.2. The numbers of the forces allocated by the signatory country to the United Nations for collective security duty or stand-by form part of the Agreement (and are included as a separate category in annex D).

6.Non-military Sanctions

6.1. The response to indirect aggression will be determined only by the Commission. Unless urgent considerations dictate otherwise, the first efforts of the Commission would be to mediate and arbitrate before deciding that some form of non-military sanctions would be necessary. All such sanctions decided upon by the Commission would be mandatory in the case of the signatory to the Agreement.

6.2. Non-military sanctions may be reinforced where the Commission decides by armed blockade with the right to search and intercept.

6.3. At the end of two years of mandatory non-military sanctions, the Commission will prepare a public report on the impact of the sanctions applied and will verify whether indirect aggression has ceased. If it has not, during the third year every effort will be made to strengthen sanctions and at the same time contingency plans will also be agreed by the Commission to allow initial preparation for the appropriate level and type of armed intervention.

6.4. By the end of the third year of mandatory sanctions a public report will be issued on progress to end the indirect aggression. If the Commission verifies that the indirect aggression continues, then the decided upon level and type of armed intervention will take place in the fourth year.

6.5. The report issued at the end of the third year of mandatory sanctions carries the status of an arbitration decision of the Commission. An appeal made by the sanctioned state against the decision of the Commission to use armed intervention to end the indirect aggression,

if it nullifies that decision or delays it by
more than a year, immediately thereafter
cancels any future obligation of the signatory
state under this Agreement. Only if the
signatory state cancels the Agreement is the
Commission released from its continuing
obligations to the signatory state.

7 Costs

7.1. In the first of the procedures by which the
signatory state can call upon the use of
collective security armed forces, costs must
be reimbursed by the signatory state. The
costs charged are budgeted total costs,
including salaries, allowances, fuel,
transportation to and from the country and
amortisation of equipment. Example daily costs
are shown in annex F for a sample mix of
troops and armaments; the costs shown apply
to the biennium printed on the annex which
will be updated.

7.2. The "Special Collective Security Contribution"
will uniquely be levied in respect of this and
all similar "Agreements" to insure against the
risk of direct armed aggression and in the
event of such an occurrence no other payment
by the signatory country will be necessary as
a reimbursement of United Nations costs. The
following formulae will be used to levy the
"Contribution":

 (i) All signatory countries commence paying the
Contribution in the tenth year from the
inaugural year of the Commission(they would
start paying in 1996 if the Commission started
operations in 1986).

(ii) The Contribution will be 4% of current defence
expenditure (and exactly 4% of the amount
obtained by applying the base period
coefficient of defence expenditure to gross
national product or public expenditure,
whichever is the smaller in the table in
paragraph 4.7.,to a three year moving average
of the chosen indicator), translated to
$U.S.at current United Nations rates. For
example if 4.5% of Gross National Product is
spent on defence in the base period the
Contribution will amount to approximately a
constant of 0.18% of the Gross National
Product in any future year.

8. <u>List of Appendices Required to Accompany a
    Disarmament Agreement</u>

A = Programme of Disarmament

B = Countries Contracted to Provide Collective
     Security for the Agreement

C = Mobilisation Timetable

D = Para-military Forces and Signatory Country
     Contribution to U.N. Forces

E = Disarmament Reference Norms(current biennium)

F = Example Costs for Packages of Armed Forces

Bibliography

Chapter 1

1) Catrina C. - "Dependence and Interdependence
    in the Global Politico Military System"
    UNIDIR Research Paper No. 1, Geneva, 1985.
2) Clairmont F.F. and Cavanagh J.H. -
    "Transnational Corporations and Global
    Markets: Changing Power Relations", in UNCTAD
    Trade and Development Review, No. 4, Winter
    1982 (E.83 II D.1), p.154.
3) Heritage Foundation (Editor Mr. B.Y. Pines)
    "A World Without A UN", Washington, D.C.,
    1984.
4) Independent Commission on International
    Development Issues -
      "North-South: a programme for Survival" Pan
      Books 1980.
      A Common Crisis: North-South Cooperation
      for World Recovery, Pan Books, 1983.
5) Prais S.J.- "The Evolution of Giant Firms in
    Britain: a Study of the Growth of
    Concentration in Manufacturing Industry in
    Britain 1909-1970", Cambridge, 1976. pp. 71
    and 249.
6) UN - "Statistical Yearbooks", 1951 and 1983.
7) UNCTAD-"Changes in International Economic
    Relations in the Last Two Decades",Trade and
    Development Review No. 5 of 1984
    (E/F.84.II.D.8).
    "Trade Links and dependency Theory", Review
    No. 6 of 1985 (E.85.II.D.20).

Chapter 2

1) Ameri,H.-"Politics and Process in the
    Specialised Agencies of the United Nations",
    Gower, Aldershot, 1982.
2) Bertrand M. - "Contribution à une reflexion
    sur la reforme des Nations Unies", Corps
    commune d'inspection (JIU/REP/85/9).
3) Cole S.-"Worlds Apart: Technology and
    North/South Relations in the Global
    Economy",UNITAR, Sussex University, 1984.
4) ICJ - Advisory Opinion, "Certain Expenses of
    the United Nations"(20 Vll 62).

5) ILO - "Report of the Committee of Experts on the Application of Conventions and Recommendations",ILO Conference 71st. Session, 1985.

6) ILO - "Report of the Director General", ILO Conference 70th. Session,1984,page 25.

7) Jackson R.- "A Study of the Capacity of the UN Development System", 2 vols. UN New York 1969 (E.70.1.1, 1970) and Resolution 2688 XXV of 1970.

8) Nicol D.and Renninger J.- "The Restructuring of the United Nations Economic and Social System: Background and analysis", Third World Quarterly, January 1982.

9) Palmer, M. - "The European Parliament", Pergamon Press, 1981.

10) Stoessinger J.G.and Associates - "Financing the United Nations System",Brookings, 1964.

11) UN - "A New United Nations Structure for Global Economic Cooperation" (E.75 II. A.7), 1975.

12) UN - "Repertory of Practice of United Nations Organs, Supplement No. 4, (ESO.V.13), 1982.

13) UN - "Report by the Secretary General,"Current Financial Crisis of the United Nations"(A/40/1102) 12 April 1986.

14) UN - "Report of the Ad hoc Committee on the Restructuring of the Economic and Social Sectors of the United Nations", GA/32/34 1978.

15) UN - "Special United Nations Fund For Economic Development (E/2381)", (1953.II B.1).

16) UN - "United Nations Conference on Trade and Employment" Final Act and Related Documents (1948. 11.D.4).

17) UNDP-"Policy Review: Coordination of Technical Cooperation at the Country Level and Examination of the Steps Taken by the UNDP to Strengthen Coordination in Practice"; Annual Report of the Administrator for 1984, DP/1985/4.

Chapter 3

1) Camps M. , Collective Management: The Reform of Global Economic Organisations New York, McGraw-Hill, 1980.

2) Coats W.R. , "The SDR as a Means of Payment: Reply to Comments," IMF Staff Papers, September 1983.

3) Commonwealth Secretariat-"Towards a New Bretton Woods: Challenges for the World Financial and Trading System", London, 1983.

4) IMF Annual Report, 1983.
5) IMF, International Monetary Reform, Washington, D.C.,1974.
6) McNamara R.-"Barbara Ward Memorial Lecture", in Anne Mattis, ed., SID Prospectus 1982 (Durham: Duke University Press, 1983).
7) Rossen S.- "Notes on Rules and Mechanisms Governing International Economic Relations",Chr. Michelsen Inst., DERAP, 1981.
8) Rothstein R.L., "Is the North-South Dialogue Worth Saving?", Third World Quarterly, January 1984.
9) Sewell J. and Zartman I.W. -"Global Negotiations: Path to the Future or Dead End Street", Third World Quarterly No 6, April 1984.
10) Stewart F. and Sengupta A.,"International Financial Cooperation: A Framework for Change",Boulder, Westview, 1982.
11) World Bank-"World Development Report" 1983.

Chapter 4

1) OECD -"Geographical Distribution of Financial Flows to Developing countries", 1982 and 1984.
2) Sen A.K.- "Poverty and Famines", Oxford, Clarendon Press, 1981.
3) UN,Joint Inspection Unit - "Reporting to the Economic and Social Council" (JIU/REP/84/7) Maurice Bertrand, Geneva 1984.
4) UN - "Medium Term Plan For the Period 1984-1989", General Assembly, Thirty-Seventh Session: Supplement No. 6. (A/37/6) 1983.
5) UN - "Population, Resources, Environment and Development", Population Studies No. 90. New York, 1984.
6) UN - "Report of the Ad Hoc Committee on the Restructuring of the Economic and Social Sectors of the United Nations System. Official Records of the General Assembly, Thirty-Second Session; Supplement No. 34A (A/32/34), 1978
7) UN-"Report of the Committee on Programme Coordination"(CPC) 24th Session Official Records (38 (A/39/38) New York 1984.
8) UNDP - "Evaluation Study NO.2 of Rural Development", June 1979.

9) UNDP – "Policy Review: Coordination of Technical Cooperation at the Country Level and Examination of the Steps Taken by the UNDP to Strengthen Coordination in Practice"; Annual Report of the Administrator for 1984, DP/1985/4.

10) UNEP –"The State of the Environment 1972-1982",Nairobi,1982.

11) UNEP – "The State of the Environment 1984", Nairobi, 1983.
    – "The State of the Environment 1985", Nairobi, 1984.

12) WHO –"Adequate Supply of Safe Water and Basic Sanitation in relation to the goal of Health For all and Primary Health Care: Review and Evaluation", WHO EB75/PC/WP/2 20 September 1984,

13) Wignaraja P.– "Entry Points in Innovative Approaches to Rural Development", in Society for International Development – "Development : Seeds of Change, Village Global Order", 1984, No. 2.

14) World Bank – "World Development Report 1984", New York, Oxford University Press.

15) World Watch Institute –"State of the World 1986", W.W. Norton and Penguin Books, Ontario, 1986.

Chapter 5

1) Ayoob M. – "Security in the Third World: the worm about to turn?",International Affairs Vol: 60: No. 1 Winter 1983/4.

2) Beker A. – "Disarmament without Order", Greenwood Press, 1985.

3) Bertrand M. – "Contribution à une reflexion sur la réforme des Nations Unies", UN Corp common d'Inspection, Genève, 1985 (JIU/REP/85/9).

4) Cutler L. N. – "The Right to Intervene", Foreign Affairs, Fall 1985.

6) Daoudi M.S. and Dajani M.S. – "Economic Sanctions: Ideals and Experience", Routledge and Kegan Paul London, 1983.

7) Ferencz B.B. – "Defining International Aggression: The Search for World Peace", Oceana publications. Vol.2. 1975.

8)   Gaule K. - "Cooperation entre les Etats
     Africains en Matiers de Dèfense" Nigerian
     Institute of International Affairs July 1981,
     Lagos, Nigeria 16)(Mimeo).
9)   ICJ - "Certain Expenses of UN" (20 VII 62).
10) Independent Commission on Disarmament and
     Security Issues - "Common Security: A
     Programme for Disarmament" Pan Books, London,
     1982.
11) Jackson R. L. - "The Non-aligned, the UN and
     the Superpowers" Council on Foreign
     Relations, Praeger 1983.
12) Jonah J.O.C. - "Disarmament and the
     Strenthening of United Nations Machinery to
     Maintain International Peace and Security",
     Disarmament, UN Vol. VII; No. 3, Autumn 1984.
13) Kemp A. - "The Third World Impact of Super
     Power Military Competition", Current Research
     on Peace and Violence, Vol. VII No. 2-3 1984.
14) Kim S.S. (Editor) - "China and the Third
     World", Westview Press, 1984.
15) Kim S.S. - "China, the United Nations and
     World Order", Princeton University Press,
     1979.
16) Maynall J. -"The Sanctions Problem in
     International Economic Relations: reflections
     in the light of experience", International
     Affairs. Vol: 60. No. 4. Autumn 1984.
17) McWhinney E. - "United Nations Law Making",
     Holmes and Meier/UNESCO Press, 1984.
18) Naidu M.V. - "Collective Security and the
     United Nations" New York, 1974.
19) Petrovsky V.F. - "The Soviet Concept of
     Security", UNIDIR 1985. Sales No. GV/E. 85
     0.2.
20) Reisman M. -"Coercion and Self-determination:
     constraining Charter Article 2(4)", American
     Journal of International Law, Vol. 78 No 3,
     1984.
21) Sherry G.L. - "Enhancing International
     Security: the Role of the United Nations",
     31st.Pugwash Conference Proceedings Report
     (Banff 1981).
22) UN - "Report of the Secretary-General on the
     Work of the Organisation", September 1982
     GA.37/1
23) UN - The Implications of Establishing an
     International Satellite Monitoring Agency",
     New York 1983, E.83.IX.3.
24) Urquhart B. - "Hammarskjold" Harper, 1972.

25)   Urquhart B. - "International Peace and
      Security", Foreign Affairs Vol. 60, No.1,
      Fall 1981.

Chapter 6

1)   Bull H. (Editor), "The Right to Intervene"
      Oxford, 1984.
2)   Mendlovitz S.-"On the Creation of a Just
      World Order: Preferred Worlds for the
      1990's", New York, The Free Press, 1977.
3)   Newcombe H.-"Nations on Record",1975;
                -"Alternative Pasts",1983.
      Peace Research Institute, Dundas, Ontario.
4)   Renninger J.P. - "ECOSOC : Options for
      Reform", UNITAR - E.81 XV PE/4, 1981.
5)   Tikhomirov V.B.-"Quantitative Analysis of
      Voting Behaviour in the General Assembly",
      UNITAR Policy and Efficacy Studies No 2 1981.
6)   UNITAR-"The United Nations and the Future",
      Proceedings of a conference in Moscow, 1974,
      published in Moscow in 1976.
7)   US Congress - "United Nations Reform",
      Committee on Foreign Relations, October 26
      1979, Washington 1980.

INDEX

absorptive capacity 14
ACC task force 80
ad hoc committee 21, 22,
    41, 96, 105, 113, 114
aggression 5, 6, 98, 99,
    106-8, 110, 115, 119,
    124, 130, 134fn(37),
    173-8
aid agencies 76, 83
appropriate technology
    70
arbitration 105,
    111,117-122, 125,
    131, 178

Bertrand 16, 27,
    41fn(1), 60, 96, 97,
    132fn(1), 161
biennial budgets 74
bilateral aid agencies
    76
block vote 23, 138, 140
Bretton Woods 52, 50,
    64fn(2), 142
budgets 25, 33-5,
    38,73, 74, 79,
    89, 148, 153, 160, 161
    Capital Development
    Fund 16

caucas meetings 23
Charter Committee 105,
    113
Charter reform 32,
    155, 159-61
China 22, 98, 104,
    109, 110, 135fn(50),
    138, 150
collective security 5,
    6, 28, 97-9, 104-10,
    121-4, 129, 131, 141,
    149, 173-5, 178-9
commission(ers) 37, 38,
    111-7, 122, 130, 157,
    160-3, 167, 173
common heritage 13
concensus 7, 11, 21,
    31, 33, 76, 112, 126,
    130, 139, 152, 163
conservation 13
consultative committee
    26, 79, 80
conventional
    disarmament 40, 98
costs 4, 10, 13, 33,
    35, 44, 44, 56, 63,
    64, 70, 73, 117,
    125-9, 171, 174, 179
CPC 77, 80, 87, 88,
    90, 91

Dadzie 19, 21-3
debt service 46, 48,
    64fn(5)
deforestation 75
desertification 21,
    69, 75
detente 2, 27, 30, 40,
    132, 143, 144, 148-9
development 4, 5, 9, 11,
    12, 18, 21, 22, 26,
    27, 29, 32, 39-41,

49, 50, 52–4, 56–8, 60, 62–3, 67–71, 73–6, 79–88, 91, 94–8, 109, 110, 115, 123, 131, 142, 147, 154, 156–9, 161, 168
DIESA 47, 52, 59, 60, 85, 93, 154
direct elections 42fn(15), 143, 145, 146, 168
Director General for Development 60, 87, 88, 154
disarmament 40, 97–100, 104, 108–10, 114, 115, 123, 124, 126, 127, 130–2, 172, 173–80
agreements 116, 126, 129
disciplinary control 21

East 4, 10, 27, 32, 53, 64, 66fn(19), 129, 136, 138, 142–8, 150, 160, 161
Economic and Social Council(ECOSOC) 25, 32, 40, 42fn(16), 55, 61, 62, 75, 79, 85, 88, 96fn(21), 136, 137, 149, 157–161, 165, 170fn(11)
economic sanctions 6, 120–2, 124, 128, 131, 135fn(49), 171
EEC 6, 37, 38, 42, 165
enforcement 6, 97, 99, 101, 105, 111, 114, 116, 117, 119, 120–5, 128, 130, 132, 133, 157, 172
environment 2, 4, 5, 11, 15fn(5), 17, 18, 21, 29, 40, 84, 95, 96, 168
European Parliament 25, 42fn(15), 157, 158
exchange rate 48, 65fn(9,12)

fact finding 104, 114, 115, 131
Falklands war 108
FAO 16, 71–3, 77, 80, 84, 96
Friendly Relations Declaration 107, 134fn(38)

GATT 20, 40, 49, 50, 54, 55, 57, 58, 60–2, 137, 142, 160, 165
General Assembly 21, 22, 24, 25, 28, 31, 32, 36, 37, 54, 55, 62, 75, 79, 81, 85, 87, 88, 90, 96, 97–106, 111–3, 115, 116, 127, 130, 133fn(23), 134fn(36, 37), 136–43, 145, 146, 149–152, 154, 156–161, 163–6, 168, 169fn(2)
global
economic management (GEM) 44, 46–50, 52–9, 61–5, 64fn(6), 87, 155, 168
economy 7, 8, 40, 42fn(21), 45, 50, 51, 58
governing bodies 26, 32, 39, 61, 66, 67, 72, 76, 77, 83, 85, 88–91, 136, 137, 154
green revolution 15fn(5)

HABITAT 18, 21, 80
health 18, 21, 29, 39, 69, 70, 72–4, 78, 80, 83, 85, 91, 95fn(7), 96fn(18), 163
for all 74, 96fn(18)
Heritage Foundation 15fn(7), 169fn(4)
heterogenity 148
Hollensteiner 71
human rights 3, 6, 7, 24, 29, 32, 38, 108,

141, 144, 151, 156,
163, 164

IAEA 24, 163
ICJ 35, 43, 101,
117-119, 133fn(17)
IFAD 16, 19, 69, 71,
74, 86, 151, 157
ILO 16, 24, 25, 38,
42fn(12), 52, 59-61,
63, 71-3, 76-8, 146,
158
IMF 40, 45, 47-61,
65fn(9,13,14), 66,
88, 120, 137, 142,
163, 166
income gaps 11
Independent Commission
15fn(9), 99, 132fn(10)
information 7, 10, 39,
72, 84, 99, 103, 104,
114-6, 120, 144, 167
insurgency 109
interdependence 4, 6,
7, 10, 15, 147
interest rates 13, 51
interference 99, 109,
156
internal disputes 106
intersectoral 153, 155
interstate disputes
140, 145
ITO 20, 166

JIU 27, 73, 87, 89,
95fn(8),
97fn(15,17,19,26),
132fn(1)
joint programming 60,
82, 85, 88

Kassebaum 150

Man and the Biosphere
84
marginal lands 75
mediation 104, 117, 131
migration 7, 8, 13, 75
mini-states 136, 139,
150, 158
minorities 6, 68

monolithism 140
multinational
companies(see TNC's)
multinational forces
124

Negotiating forums 20
NGO's 30, 158
NIEO 12, 139
non-aligned 28, 110,
138, 143-9, 169fn(1)
Nordic Group 104
North 4, 10, 12, 19, 27,
32, 34, 35, 45, 53,
55, 64, 136, 138,
141-3, 146-151, 160,
161, 167
nuclear arms 5, 28,
40, 97

OECD 8, 9, 94fn(2)
OPEC 20

Palme 99, 106, 122
participation 14, 22,
23, 30, 39, 63, 84,
95fn(7), 115, 139,
145, 161
peace-keeping 17, 35, 36,
99, 101, 103-5, 110,
112, 114, 117, 119,
121, 122, 128, 130,
133fn(32), 157, 159,
162, 171, 173
peaceful settlement of
disputes 14, 20, 27,
38, 99, 103, 111,
114, 116, 118,
133fn(32)
permanent members 22, 23,
25, 32, 41, 98-100,
104-6, 109-11, 113,
116, 129, 133fn(8),
136, 137, 141-3, 156,
159, 160, 168
planning cycle 79, 80,
87, 93, 154
policy coordination
79, 153-5
primary health care
21, 69, 70, 73, 74,

80, 91, 97, 163, <u>see</u>
<u>also</u> health
process 2, 23, 24, 26,
  27, 29-32, 42fn(18),
  50, 52-6, 58, 59, 61,
  68, 73, 99, 103,
  117-9, 124, 131, 139,
  144, 149, 165, 167
Programme Committees 90
protectionism 8, 30,
  56, 58
public education 39,
  164-5

Reagonomics 102
redistribution 11, 12
regional
  alliances 110
  blocks 136, 158, 160
  Economic Commission 10
  Seas Programme 16
resident
  coordinators
  26, 81, 82, 86, 92,
  155
  representative
  UNDP(RRUNDP) 81-3,
  85, 86, 91, 114, 115,
  128, 171
restructuring 20, 21,
  41fn(4), 44, 49, 53,
  61, 64fn(1), 79, 94,
  95fn(12), 156, 160
revolution 7, 15, 109,
  165
rural development 18,
  21, 27, 40, 67-71,
  73, 75, 76, 79-87,
  91, 94, 95, 96
rural poor 70

SDR <u>see</u> Special
  Drawing Rights
Secretariat 20-1, 24,
  26, 33, 35, 37, 38,
  51, 52, 54-63, 67,
  73, 78-80, 85, 86,
  88, 89, 94, 100, 105,
  111, 113-5, 117, 119,
  121, 123, 129, 131,
  137, 140, 152, 155,

157, 162-3, 167
Secretary General
  29,35-8, 43, 83, 89,
  97, 102-4, 113-6,
  127, 133fn(22,32),
  135fn(48), 138, 145,
  159
Security Council 20, 22,
  23, 25, 28, 31, 32,
  37, 41, 42fn(16), 62,
  97-107, 109-22, 125,
  126, 128-35, 137,
  138, 141-3, 147-9,
  156, 157, 159-62,
  171, 173
SID 64
soil erosion 5, 69, 75
South 4, 10, 19, 27,32,
  35, 42, 45, 53, 55,
  136-8, 142, 146-50,
  160, 161
sovereignty 23, 108,
  124
Soviet Union (USSR) 22,
  28, 31, 102, 103,
  106, 133fn(17,19),
  138, 143
Special Drawing Rights
  48, 51, 55, 60,
  65fn(11,13,15)
specialised agencies 19,
  20, 22, 32, 34, 36,
  42fn(18), 52, 67,
  71-3, 75, 83, 86-8,
  90, 136, 143, 158,
  161, 165
structural adjustments
  40, 50, 56, 57, 155
subversion 5, 6, 28,
  109, 121, 122, 124,
  134
SUNFED 20
superpowers 5, 6, 14,
  22, 28, 31, 40, 99,
  103, 107, 109, 111,
  117, 132, 133, 135,
  143, 146, 148, 149,
  161, 169fn(1)
supranational 25, 62,
  162, 163
surveillance 65, 115

technical cooperation
17, 21, 39, 42fn(17),
61, 66, 71–3, 76, 78,
81, 83, 84, 86, 88,
91–3, 95fn(10),
96fn(23), 154, 155,
163
terrorism 5, 98
terrorist 107, 130,
175
Third World 6, 7, 28,
29, 40, 50, 58, 68,
69, 95, 97–9, 102,
106–10, 112, 113,
121, 123, 126,
129–32, 166
traditional farmers
15fn(5)
transnational
corporations(TNC's)
16, 76

UNCTAD 8, 9, 15fn(3),
20, 38, 40, 49,
52–62, 160, 166
UNDP 16, 20, 24–6,
42fn(17), 61,
66fn(23), 67, 71–3,
76, 77, 81–3, 85, 88,
93, 94fn(1),
95fn(7,9),
96fn(22,23,27), 114,
137, 154, 157, 161
UNEP 95, 96, 158, 16,
69, 75, 80, 82, 84, 87
UNESCO 16, 18, 84, 144
UNICEF 71, 72, 76–8,
81, 83, 85, 157
UNIDIR 15, 102
UNIDO 16, 54, 60, 61,
63, 78, 87
UNITAR
169fn(7), 170fn(8–11)
United States(US) 5, 12,
22, 24, 28, 36, 38,
45–7, 53, 63, 103,

104, 138, 147, 148,
150
Uniting for Peace
Resolution 22, 101,
106, 112
USSR (see Soviet Union)

verification 24, 39,
111, 115, 116, 163,
175
Veto 22, 23, 25, 37, 41,
97, 100, 102, 104–6,
109, 111, 119, 130,
132fn(8), 137, 138,
142, 159–161
voluntary funding 24,
71, 136, 137, 139
voting structures 32,
86, 150

water 5, 21, 27, 38,
74, 80, 83, 96, 131
Decade 83, 96
WCARRD Conference 82,
84
weighted voting 49, 53,
66(fn16), 86, 142,
150–2, 158, 160, 161,
166, 171
West 10, 11, 27, 32, 34,
35, 53, 64, 66fn(19),
138, 141, 142–51, 160
WHO 16, 18, 39,
71–2, 76, 78,
81, 85, 89, 94, 95,
163
World Bank 49, 50,
52–5, 58, 66fn(23),
71–2, 77, 87, 93, 96,
120, 137,
142, 157 161, 166
Group 45, 52, 53, 55,
56, 59–61, 86, 121,
137, 142, 155, 157,
161, 162